STUDY GUIDE

NEIL T. ANDERSON
& ROBERT L. SAUCY

HARVEST HOUSE PUBLISHERS
EUGENE, OREGON 97402

Cover by Left Coast Design, Portland, Oregon

THE COMMON MADE HOLY STUDY GUIDE
Copyright © 1997 by Harvest House Publishers
Eugene, Oregon 97402

ISBN 1-56507-760-1

Printed in the United States of America.
97 98 99 00 01 02 / BP / 10 9 8 7 6 5 4 3 2 1

Contents

Before You Begin

Being made holy. It's God's will, His desire, His plan for you. But exactly how does holiness happen? What is your role and what is God's role? What can you do to work with the Potter? What does it take to make yourself moldable in His hands?

The process of becoming holy is a process of grace. God does the work in us as we open ourselves to His refining touch. We do so with choices about how we spend our time, what we think about, which activities we are involved in, whom we worship and fellowship with, and how we pray.

Simply reading about such things as abiding in Christ, being filled with the Spirit, growing in holiness through fellowship, and the warfare of sanctification is not the same as starting to live out these things. It is our hope that this guide will help you start putting into practice what you have read about in *The Common Made Holy*.

As you work through these lessons, you'll be studying the Scriptures closely and, we pray, opening yourself to the work of God in your life. We encourage you to linger over the passages of Scripture and let God do His transforming work in you.

May this be an opportunity for you to draw closer to your loving and powerful heavenly Father, the Potter who does indeed desire to make you holy.

—Neil Anderson and Robert Saucy

God's Desire for You

• Why did you pick up the book *The Common Made Holy*? What do you hope to learn?

• What transformation do you hope to experience as a result of studying God's truth as revealed in His Word and set forth in this book?

The Potter's Plan

• Review the metaphorical retelling of the Creation, the Fall, the Incarnation, and the Resurrection on pages 7-10. What truth(s) does this retelling powerfully illustrate for you?

- What new or greater understanding of the enemy's role in your life and his goal in this world did you gain from this story?

- What do you appreciate more about God's eternal plan as a result of reading this account?

- What do you appreciate more about God's desire for you as a result of reading about the Potter's plan?

The Potter's Work

This book is about the common made holy by the hands of God. The theological term for this change is *sanctification*. Although God's redeemed pots have many other useful purposes for remaining on planet earth, nothing is more important to the Potter than to have them—to have you—free from their awful past and made pure like Him.

- At this point of the study, how do you define *sanctification*? What definitions have you heard? What Scripture passages, if any, come to mind when you think about sanctification?

- In whose life have you seen God do His work of sanctification? Describe some of the changes you saw Him work in that person's life. What did that person do to cooperate with God's plan for his/her sanctification, to open him/herself to God's transforming touch?

God's primary concern isn't your career choice, whether you're a carpenter, plumber, or engineer. His primary concern is what kind of carpenter, plumber, or engineer you are. God's priorities are character before career and maturity before ministry.

• How has God used your career choice—or perhaps the sacrifice of a career path—to make you more like Christ?

• When have you seen God's concern for maturity before ministry and church purity before church growth reflected in a real-life situation? Be specific about the work God was doing and the response of the people involved.

In this book, we are going to show the necessity for growth and then attempt to define sanctification. We hope to show how God intends for us to conform to His image. The world, the flesh, and the devil will pull out all the stops and make every effort to stop this process in our life, but we are committed to helping you understand God's desire for you to grow in Christ.

• Read Colossians 1:27 in context. Why do you think this verse is key to *The Common Made Holy*?

• Sanctification is the work God does in the life of His children. Have you made the decision to let God be God? Do you desire nothing more than to be the person He created you to be? In a few sentences, state your commitment. If you haven't yet made that commitment, now is a good time. Simply confess your sin (Romans 3:23): tell God that you are aware of how you have fallen short of His standards for you. Receive His forgiveness (1 John 1:9) and acknowledge that His forgiveness comes through the death of His Son on the cross for your sin (John 3:16). Thank God for this sacrifice and invite Jesus to be Lord of your life (Romans 10:9).

• The will of God is good, acceptable, and perfect for you (Romans 12:2), but His plan may also involve some times of testing in order that you may be purified. Read 1 Peter 4:12-14 again and think back on a period of testing in your life. Looking back, what can you now appreciate about the work God was doing in your life and your heart? Be specific.

The Refiner's fire is necessary in order for the Potter to conform His earthen vessels back into His image. You will be tempted to believe it isn't worth it, but indeed it is. You have been chosen by the King of kings and Lord of lords to be His child and set aside from all other creation to do His will, which is good, acceptable, and perfect.

Almighty and Creator God, I am humbled and awed by the fact that You breathed Your divine life into this clay pot . . . that You sent Your holy Son to redeem my fallen nature . . . and that nothing is more important to You than my becoming more like Jesus. I can best respond in the songwriter's words—"My heart's desire,/ Is to be holy/ Set apart unto You my Maker/ Ready to do Your will."[1] I look forward to what You will teach me and the sanctifying, transforming work You will do in me. I look forward to being made holy like You. I pray in Jesus' name. Amen.

The COMMON MADE HOLY

1

Designed for Holiness

We human beings are created by God to play a significant role in our spiritual growth. This capacity to participate in the shaping of our own lives is rooted in the biblical truth that we are created in "the image of God" (Genesis 1:26,27).

• In a limited sense, God has called each of us to participate in the development of what He intends us to become. How have God-given abilities, social opportunities, personal choices, and hard work gotten you to the point where you are today?

Created with the capacity to think, we are intricately involved in the process of shaping ourselves and determining our destiny:

Whoever sows a thought, reaps an action;
Whoever sows an action, reaps a habit;
Whoever sows a habit, reaps a lifestyle;
Whoever sows a lifestyle, reaps a destiny.

• What thoughts, actions, and habits have you sown in regards to your spiritual lifestyle and destiny? Be specific about the positives as well as the negatives.

The Biblical Challenge to Grow (16)*

The sovereign grace of God and human responsibility are intertwined catalysts for human growth and potential.

Review the parables of the talents (Matthew 25:14-20) and the pounds (Luke 19:12-27).

- According to these stories Jesus told, what is your responsibility when it comes to your personal and spiritual growth?

- According to John 15:5 and 2 Peter 1:3, what does God provide for your spiritual growth?

- What challenges to grow do you find in the following passages?
  2 Corinthians 10:15

Ephesians 2:21,22

Ephesians 4:16

---

* The subtitles refer to corresponding sections in the book *The Common Made Holy*. Page references are in parentheses.

1 Thessalonians 5:11

1 Peter 2:2

2 Peter 3:18

Jude 20

• Our growth is in every dimension of salvation, but especially in our faith and knowledge of Christ. According to Ephesians 4:13, what is the ultimate outcome of this growth?

Believers are growing toward a destiny characterized by the fullness of Christ's life and character (*see* Colossians 1:28 and 3:10). It is God's plan to restore a fallen humanity to its original design. He will faithfully do His part, but what if we don't shoulder our responsibility?

Recognizing True Spiritual Growth (18)

If we make doctrine or knowledge an end in itself we will distort the very purpose for which it was intended. Jesus said that the greatest commandments are to " 'love the Lord your God with all your heart and with all your soul and with all your mind' . . . [and] 'love your neighbor as yourself' " (Matthew

22:37,39). Proper biblical instruction should result in all of us falling in love with God and each other.

• Who in your life models a person who has grown in the knowledge of God and His likeness? What was key to this person maturing spiritually rather than merely growing old physically?

• Looking at your life through this lens, what growth do you sense in yourself? What actions and/or attitudes reflect a deeper love for God? For other people? Be specific.

It's possible for a person to master the Bible's content and not even be a Christian.

• When, if ever, has that statement described you? When did you, like zealous Saul, come to know Jesus Christ as Savior and begin to love Him as Lord?

• In 1 Peter 3:15, the apostle writes, "Always be prepared to give an answer to everyone who asks you to give the reason for the hope that you have." What are you doing to become more familiar with God's Word and the truth presented there?

• What are you doing to keep from reducing your Bible study to an intellectual exercise? More positively, what are you doing to personally appropriate God's Word so that the Spirit can use it to make you more like Jesus?

We can develop our skills, exercise our gifts, and learn better ways to become Christian leaders, yet still miss the mark (1 Corinthians 13:1,2). Jesus said, "By this all men will know that you are my disciples, if you love one another" (John 13:35).

Viewing God's Holiness (21)

Every child of God begins his or her spiritual pilgrimage as a babe in Christ. Despite our unique personality, gifts, and talents, we all hold in common one pursuit: We are to be holy as God is holy (1 Peter 1:16).

To speak of God's holiness is to speak of His distinctness or His separateness from all other things. As such, God is also separate from all the evil and moral pollution which defiles the creation. The meaning of holiness climaxes with God's separateness from sin.

• What greater understanding or appreciation of holiness do you have after reading this section?

• Look at Exodus 33:18-20 and Isaiah 6:1-7. In light of this discussion of holiness, comment on how Moses and Isaiah responded to the glory of God.

Nothing can so immediately and profoundly affect the character and behavior of mankind more than to be confronted with the glory of God, which is a manifestation of His presence.

• How might you be affected by such a confrontation with the glory of God?

• What do you do to live actively aware of God's constant presence in your life? What does—or would—this awareness do to your sense of your own sin?

The psalmist declared, "Worship the Lord in the splendor of his holiness; tremble before him, all the earth" (96:9). If, like Isaiah or Peter, we were brought into the Lord's presence, we would indeed tremble and crumble at His feet with an overwhelming conviction of His holiness and our sinfulness.

Set Apart for God (24)

Because God is holy, everything associated with Him is also holy or sanctified. Frequently throughout Scriptures, God reminds His people that they are to be holy because they belong to Him who is holy (Leviticus 19:2; 11:44; 20:7, 20:26; 1 Peter 1:16).

Uses of the word *holy* in the Old Testament show that things are marked off as related to God without any moral or ethical implications, but there was also an emphasis on holiness in the moral and ethical sphere.

• To what does the word *holy* refer in the following passages? Where does *holy* refer to the moral and ethical sphere?

Leviticus 11:43-47

Leviticus 16:30

Psalm 24:3,4

- Explain how cleanliness or purity is an aspect of the broader concept of holiness.

Consider the world we live in and how the line between holy and profane or common is often ignored.
- Give some examples of how the world treats some things which are holy as though they are common.

- What holy thing(s), if any, are you treating as common?

For God's people to live in sin was to profane God's name before others (Proverbs 30:9; Ezekiel 36:20-23).

Called to Be Holy (26)

We who name Jesus as Savior and Lord are called to be holy. But obviously we can't become holy like God apart from the grace of God. We can't become holy outside of an intimate relationship with God's Son.

Jesus said, "This is eternal life, that they may know Thee, the only true God, and Jesus Christ whom Thou hast sent" (John 17:3 NASB).
- To know a person in this sense is not to have mere knowledge about that person; rather, it is to know that person as a friend—to be in an intimate relationship so that your lives influence each other. In what specific ways does Jesus, your Savior and Friend, influence your daily life?

- What instructions for living in a way that pleases God do you find in the following passages?
  2 Corinthians 7:1

  1 Thessalonians 5:19-23

  1 Peter 1:14-16

The importance of holiness in the believer's life is evident in the way that holiness is linked to life itself.
- What does Paul teach about this relationship between holiness and life itself in Romans 8:13 and Romans 6:21,22?

- Between the initial salvation of being set free from sin and the final state of eternal life there is the process of growth in holiness or sanctification. What do these passages teach about the process and the end of sanctification?
  2 Thessalonians 2:13

  Hebrews 12:14

- Clearly Scripture reveals that God has called us to be holy as He is holy. Without this holiness, we will die in hell. But, humanly speaking, why should we be holy? What pleasure is there in living a holy life? What personal benefit is there in being a saint?

• Explain how the commandments of God are not restrictive but protective. When did you first learn this lesson for yourself?

• Why do we need to be protected from self-centered living? From the gods of this world? What results from self-centered living and following the world? What are two or three examples of specific commands by which God offers us the protection we need?

There is nothing inherently wrong with a new car or house, fame and fortune, an earthly title or an academic degree. But these and other rewards of the world will not give us what a Spirit-filled life of holiness can. The unknown author of the following lines realized this truth and the good gifts God had given him even though they were gifts he hadn't originally requested. Look at your own life through the lens of this poem.

I asked God for strength, that I might achieve;
    I was made weak, that I might learn humbly to obey.
I asked for health, that I might do greater things;
    I was given infirmity, that I might do better things.
I asked for riches, that I might be happy;
    I was given poverty, that I might be wise.
I asked for power, that I might have the praise of men;
    I was given weakness, that I might feel the need of God.

I asked for all things, that I might enjoy life;
I was given life that I might enjoy all things.

I got nothing I asked for, but everything I hoped for;
Almost despite myself, my unspoken prayers were answered.
I am among all men, most richly blessed!

• Make the second line of each couplet specific with details from your experience. When, for instance, did you learn obedience from a time of weakness? When did you do better things because of an infirmity?

• Now close with some thanksgiving. What blessings has God given you, some of them perhaps in spite of your prayers?

So how do we grow in holiness or sanctification? What part do we play and what part does God play? What means does God use in our sanctification? Is growing difficult or easy? What helps us grow or hinders us from growing? These questions and others are all part of understanding how we grow as Christians—or, how the common is made holy.

Creator and Holy God, it is amazing to consider that You made me in Your image and that You call me to be holy as You are holy. I thank You that when You call, You empower: that You will work in my life to make me more loving, to enable me to obey Your commandments, to transform my life by Your Spirit. Help me to be responsive and responsible for my personal and spiritual growth so that You might freely do the sanctifying work in my life which You would do. I pray in the name of Jesus, through whom this process is made possible. Amen.

The
COMMON
MADE
Holy

2

Being Saved and Sanctified

Slavery in the United States was abolished by the Thirteenth Amendment on December 18, 1865. How many slaves were there on December 19? In reality, none, but many still lived like slaves.

• When you first read this bit of American history, at what point did you realize the metaphorical and theological implications for you?

• In what ways are you, like some of those freed slaves, continuing to live in bondage to sin even though you have been set free by Christ's death on the cross (Romans 6:11)? More specifically, in what areas of your life are you doing the same things you have always done and feeling the same way you have always felt—and therefore concluding you must not really be free and continuing to live like a slave?

- What message does God have for you personally in this metaphorical retelling of the good news that Jesus Christ died for your sins and that you have been set free in Him—even if you don't feel like and may not even act like it?

If we want to mature in our relationship with God, then we need to understand the difference between what Christ has already accomplished for us and what still needs to be done. We also need to know what part Christ plays in our sanctification and what part we play.

Understanding the Gospel (33)

The idea of salvation in the Old Testament meant "to be roomy or broad" and carried the sense of being rescued.[1] The idea of salvation in the New Testament carries over the meaning of deliverance and freedom (*see* Galatians 5:1) and communicates the notion of wholeness, soundness, and health. Holiness is not just getting rid of sin. Rather, holiness is freeing us from all the hindrances that would prevent us from being all that we were created to be.

What Adam and Eve lost as a result of their sin was life. They died spiritually—that is, they lost their relationship with God and became slaves to sin. Every person since that time has been born physically alive but spiritually dead.

- When did you first become aware of your sinfulness, your spiritual deadness, your separation from God? What prompted that realization?

- Before coming to a saving knowledge of Jesus Christ, what did you turn to in your quest for significance? How did you answer the questions "Who am I?" and "Why am I here?"

- What identity did you derive from your physical appearance, social status, and the roles you played? When did you come to the point of agreeing with Solomon—"Meaningless! Meaningless! . . . Utterly meaningless! Everything is meaningless" (Ecclesiastes 1:2)?

The church in the western world has presented Jesus as the Messiah who died for our sins. If we will receive Him into our hearts, He will forgive us our sins and we will get to go to heaven when we die.

- Summarize what is wrong with that presentation of the above gospel message. What truth about eternal life and about salvation is missing? (See page 35.)

- What do the following verses teach about the first aspect of the twofold purpose of Christ's coming?
  John 16:11

  Colossians 1:13,14

1 John 3:8

Jesus came to offer us the way back into relationship with God. He also died on the cross so that we "may have life, and have it to the full" (John 10:10)—and He was talking about our spiritual life, which is our relationship with God. Jesus was talking about a redeemed humanity that is fully alive in Christ.

Salvation Is Past, Present, and Future (36)

Both salvation and sanctification are presented in Scripture in the past, present, and future verb tenses. In this chapter, we'll look at salvation. The Bible says we have been saved, we are presently being saved, and we will someday be fully saved.

- Explain the past tense or "have been saved" aspect of our salvation. See John 11:25; Ephesians 2:4,5,8; 2 Timothy 1:8,9; and Titus 3:4,5.

Every child of God has experienced (past tense) salvation. Because of our belief in Jesus Christ, we are now spiritually alive and will remain so even when we die physically.

Scripture also tells us we are presently "being saved."

- Summarize this present tense aspect of our salvation. See 1 Corinthians 1:18; 2 Corinthians 2:15; and Philippians 2:12.

- We do not work for our salvation, but we are called to work out what God has born in us. What does it mean to work out our salvation? What are you doing so that God can conform you to the image of His Son? Be specific.

Our salvation begins on earth, but it is completed in heaven. That is why Scripture speaks about a future aspect of salvation: we will someday be fully saved.

- What aspect of our salvation is reserved for the future? What have we not yet been saved from but know that we will be? See Romans 5:9,10; Romans 13:11; Hebrews 9:28; and Ephesians 1:13,14.

Just like salvation, the biblical concept of sanctification carries us all the way from our new birth in Christ to the final perfection of glorification. In the next chapter, we are going to identify and explain the three tenses of the believer's sanctification.

Almighty God, I thank You for the grace and mercy revealed in Your plan of salvation. Thank You that You have saved me in Christ and His death on the cross. Thank You that You are saving me and that I am privileged and empowered by You to be a partner in that process as I work out my salvation. And thank You that You will one day save me from the wrath of Your future judgment. Yours is indeed amazing grace and I thank You for it in Jesus' name. Amen.

Being Made Holy

Every living organism suffers through the three progressive stages of birth, growth, and maturation. Each stage has its own contribution, characteristic, scope, and limits as to what it can supply in the overall purpose of the organism.

Who or what a person, animal, or plant will be is established at birth. From that stage on, no creature or plant can be anything other than what the Creator intended if it is going to fulfill its purpose.

- What encouragement about your spiritual growth do you find in this fact?

- Growth in your relationship with God calls for you to put off childish things. What childish things have you—or do you need to—put off so that you can grow spiritually?

Just as there are three tenses to our salvation, there are three tenses to our sanctification. Let's now look more closely at how

God has made us holy, continues to make us holy, and ultimately assures us of perfect holiness.

Past-Tense Sanctification (40)

Past-tense sanctification is often spoken of as positional sanctification because it speaks of the holy position or status that the believer has "in Christ."

Just as the past tense reality of salvation is the basis for the present tense working out of our salvation, so also is our position in Christ the basis for our growth in Christ.

- What does 2 Peter 1:3,4 teach about the positional truth of who we are in Christ? See also 1 Corinthians 1:2 and 6:19 and Hebrews 10:10.

Explain why this position of being holy because we are "in Christ" is the basis for our growing in sanctification.

Sinner or Saint? (41)

The New Testament describes believers as "saints," which means "holy ones" (Romans 1:7, Philippians 1:1). Being a saint does not necessarily reflect a person's present measure of growth in character, but it does identify those who are rightly related to God. (The New Testament offers plenty of evidence that a believer is capable of sinning, but it never clearly identifies the believer as a sinner.)

- Explain how the word "saint" is used in the New Testament. How is it opposed to "sinner"? What is its relationship to "called" or "elect"?

- What is a saint's relationship to sin?

- We are saints who sin, but in Christ, we have all the resources we need in order not to sin. What are some of those resources? Why are these resources key to present-tense sanctification?

Made Holy Through Christ (44)

Believing faith joins us to Christ so that we now share in all that Christ is, including His holiness (1 Corinthians 1:30).

- Explain how the Old Testament high priest—his duties and his actions—foreshadowed the perfect priest we have in Jesus.

- Why are we New Testament believers able to enter God's holy presence?

What About Sin? (46)

As believers, we still have the capacity to sin when we choose to believe Satan's lies and walk according to the flesh.

- Explain the difference between "having" sin and "being" basically sinful by nature. Why is this distinction significant?

• What encouragement and hope do you find in the truth of Hebrews 10:14,19-22?

• Why does—or should—the fact that you are children of God motivate you toward holy living rather than give you license to sin?

Those who understand they are children of God and have their hope fixed on Jesus purify themselves (1 John 3:3). They live according to who they really are—children of God.

Present-Tense Sanctification (47)

God performed a gracious work when He called us out of darkness into His marvelous light and granted us the status of holiness by virtue of our union with Christ. He did this so that He could carry on His work of making us holy.

The process of growing from carnality to Christlikeness is known as present-tense sanctification, or progressive sanctification (Romans 6:22).

• Define justification and sanctification by describing what aspect of sin each is related to. (The words of the Westminster Catechism and theologian Louis Berkhof [pages 47 and 48 respectively] are helpful.)

• At the moment we became justified and sanctified positionally, the Spirit of God came into our lives and began the process of transforming our character. What do the following passages teach about your role in that process?

2 Corinthians 7:1

1 Thessalonians 4:3

Hebrews 12:14

Conforming to God's Image (49)

The concept of being made holy is a dominant theme of Scripture. Terms like "growth," "edification," "building up," "transformation," "purification," and "renewing" refer to the process of conforming to the image of God.

- Read Colossians 2:6,7. What does this passage reveal about being conformed to the image of God? What is the key first step? What have you done—or do you need to do—to become "firmly rooted" in Christ? What do you need to do to stay firmly rooted in Him—and why is that connection essential to spiritual growth?

- Look again at 1 John 2:12-14. Where do you see yourself in John's three stages of Christian growth? Are you a little child, a young man, or a father in the faith? Explain your answer.

- Who are you as a child of God? What does that status mean for how you are able to live your life? For the process of sanctification God has planned for you? Put differently, how can not understanding what it means to be God's child interfere with, if not completely block, your growth into Christlikeness?

A Key Clarification (51)

In Colossians, Paul affirmed both past- and present-tense sanctification.

• What is the danger of emphasizing past-tense sanctification over the fact that we sin even when we are believers?

• What is the danger of emphasizing present-tense sanctification over the truth that Christ has made us complete (Colossians 2:10)?

• What is a biblical balance between the truth of past-tense sanctification and the necessity of present-tense sanctification?

The New Man: Becoming Fully Human (51)

Becoming holy is not simply about being conformed to the likeness of God. It is also about being made fully human. Sanctification is the process through which God makes us the whole human beings He created us to be.

- To be human as God created us is to exist in the image of God. Give some specific examples (perhaps from your own life) of how sin has distorted, if not utterly destroyed, that image.

- How did you respond to the statements of Maximos the Confessor and J.I. Packer on page 52? What new appreciation do you have for your humanness and God's plan?

- Why is holiness "about the celebration of our humanity"[1]?

Sanctification is somber in the sense that it involves the death of the old sinful life so that the new life can spring forth. But there's great joy in becoming holy because we're entering into the fullness of our humanity!

Future-Tense Sanctification (53)

As Paul explained in Ephesians 5:25-27, at salvation, Christ set us apart to Himself that He might finally make us perfectly holy.
- What ultimate goal for believers is reflected in 1 Thessalonians 3:12,13 and 5:23,24?

Read Philippians 1:6.

• What "good work" has God begun in you? Be specific about any progress you sense in your present-day sanctification.

• In light of that fact that you, a saint, still choose to sin, what hope do you find in this verse?

The destiny of believers is to share in the glory of God—to "be conformed to the likeness of [His] Son" (Romans 8:29) and to "bear the image of the heavenly [man, or Jesus]" (1 Corinthians 15:49).

The Scope of Sanctification (54)

Scripture reveals to us that becoming holy is all-encompassing. It involves the transformation of every facet of our being.

Like growth in the natural realm, healthy spiritual growth involves growth in every part in proper balance.

• According to Romans 12:2, Ephesians 4:24, and Colossians 3:10, what will characterize a sanctified mind?

• According to Romans 12:2, what will characterize a sanctified will?

- According to Romans 8:13,23 and 1 Corinthians 6:19,20, what will characterize a sanctified body?

- Look again at the words of Charles Hodge (pages 54-55). What does this passage help you realize about the importance of balance in your spiritual growth? What kind of imbalance in your own spiritual growth, if any, are you currently aware of?

- What are you doing to put yourself in a position where God can do His transforming work in your spirit, your will, and your body? What decisions are you making to help His work take place in your life?

Sanctification flows from the new heart of the believer, and since the heart is the center of the person out of which all life flows, true sanctification cannot help but touch every area of life.

Almighty and holy God, I am awed and humbled by Your plan to sanctify me, to make me holy as You are holy. I am so aware of my propensity to sin. . . . Yet I am also aware of Your forgiveness. I thank You for that forgiveness and for the process of sanctification, past, present, and future. Teach me what it means to live as a child of God. Guide me in my choices that I may know the joy of entering the fullness of my humanity. And continue in me the good work You have begun to conform me to the likeness of Christ, in whose name I pray. Amen.

A Changed Relationship

Sin separates man from a holy God. However, there are two orientations people have to sin that are diametrically opposite to each other, and both are debilitating.

First, some people seem to have no moral conscience or any awareness of their own sin (Jeremiah 6:15); they have no relationship with God. Second is the orientation of people who have a relationship with God but who cannot seem to accept His forgiveness for their sin.

• Are you overwhelmed with your sin and unable to accept God's forgiveness? To what degree are you trapped by legalism? Are you trying to earn God's favor by doing good? Support your answers with evidence from your life.

• At what points, if any, can you identify with the missionary whose words appear on page 58? Consider both the "before" and "after" aspects of his experience.

By God's grace, you too can realize that you are "a saint who has chosen to sin" and become "free of Satan's bondage and aware of the lies he has been feeding [you]."

The True Nature of Sin (59)

Growth in the Christian life is totally dependent upon God's graceful presence in our lives; therefore, to grow we must be rightly related to Him. This requires dealing with the reality of sin.

It is difficult to grasp the true nature of sin for several reasons.

We have always been personally involved in sin and therefore cannot fully grasp the difference between sin and perfect righteousness. Because of our finiteness, we simply cannot understand sin in its full depth.

Our understanding is skewed because of our own sinfulness.

Our awareness of what is sinful grows dull with tolerance and exposure to sin.

No human has yet experienced the full weight of sin's consequences.

• Which of these reasons has most affected your inability to fully understand sin in all its awfulness?

- More specifically, what sins do you tend to rationalize rather than confess?

- What sin—both personal and societal—have you become tolerant of because of your exposure to it?

- What might a glimpse of hell do to your attitude toward sin?

- What does looking at the cross of Christ tell you about the true nature of sin?

Scripture not only shows the heinousness of sin, but also reveals it as a power superior over all human effort.
- In what area(s) of your life have you felt—or do you feel—the "reign" of sin (Romans 5:21)? Be specific about your struggle.

- Why can't education, the practice of moral disciplines, or psychology help us overcome sin?

Sin is a power that enslaves us. Only the superior power of God in Christ can redeem us from the reigning power of sin (Romans 7:24,25).

A Relationship Broken by Sin (61)

The relationship Adam and Eve had with God at creation is the intended "natural" state of humanity—living in fellowship with God. Sin, however, broke this relationship.

The original sin of Adam and Eve reveals the essence of what sin is: the desire to play god over our own life.

- Consider sins that you struggle or have struggled with. In each instance, what temptation to exercise your own will independent of God do you face? Put differently, what choice about what is right and what is wrong are you making?

- What consequences have you faced as a result of the rebellion toward God you just identified? Be as specific as possible especially about the bondage to sin you have experienced.

- What have you done to try to gain acceptance, security, and significance apart from God? Consider negative attitudes as well as actions which hurt you and others.

A Change in Our Legal Relationship (62)

Fellowship with God and others is experienced by living according to the laws of His moral order. We might say that sin is a breaking of our "legal relationship" with God. We are guilty of breaking His laws and therefore no longer stand in a right relationship with Him.

• According to Galatians 3:10 and 22, what do we as law-breakers face?

• Besides coming under God's judgment or condemnation for our sin, we experience the pollution and corruption of sin. According to 2 Corinthians 6:14 and Psalm 24:3,4, what further consequence of our sin does that pollution cause?

Restoring the Relationship (64)

God demonstrates His incredible love when He takes the initiative to restore a person's relationship with Him. The fault lies entirely with the sin of the person, but God nevertheless sends His own Son to bring a sinner back into fellowship.

• Review the story which opens this section (page 64). What does this illustration help you understand about sin, yourself, and/or God?

• Now review Romans 3:21-26 and then summarize its teaching on each of the following points:
Whose righteousness provides the basis for God to declare us right? See verses 21 and 22.

By whom is God's righteousness made available to us sinners? See verse 24.

Define "grace." What does Romans 3:23 teach about God's grace?

According to verses 22,26,30, what must we do to receive our justification or right standing before God?

The Results of Our Restoration (67)

The change of legal relationship brought about by God's gracious gift of justification provides results that are absolutely essential as a foundation for life with God, which is the only means to growth and sanctification (Romans 5:1-3). Consider now two fruits of justification which provide the basis for growth in the Christian life.

- First, explain the significance of the past tense verb in the clause "we have been justified through faith" (Romans 5:1).

- What freedom can you experience because the punishment for your sin has already fallen on Christ? See 1 John 4:18.

- *Peace with God*: Are you motivated to living a holy life by threat of hurt or by love borne out of gratitude for what God has done for you? Explain.

- What did you learn from my (Neil's) account of being dismissed from school to help pick corn rather than as a punishment for skipping religious day instruction? What is keeping you from running to your heavenly Father (Ephesians 3:12)?

- *Access to God*: Why is the fact that you, who have been justified through the gift of God's righteousness in Christ, have access to God such good news?

A Change in Our Personal Moral Relationship (71)

In addition to the change in legal relationship which takes place in justification, there is a change in what might be called personal moral relationship, a change which is foundational for Christian growth. The change that allows us who are unholy and polluted by sin to have fellowship with a holy God is most often called positional sanctification.

- According to Galatians 2:20 and Romans 6:11, what is the specific change we refer to as "positional" or "definitive" sanctification?

• What do the following passages teach about definitive sanctification and its results in our life?
Galatians 3:26-29

Galatians 4:6,7

Hebrews 10:19,22

Our justification through Christ's righteous obedience removes the condemnation from the guilt of sin, and our sanctification in Christ's holiness makes it possible to walk in fellowship with God.

Recognizing Our New Identity (73)

Peace with and acceptance by God make it possible for us to experience practical sanctification. Because we as Christians are no longer at enmity with God and are free from the fear of His condemning judgment, we can enjoy a relationship in which we are conformed more and more into His likeness.

• This growth cannot take place if we still see our selves as slaves of sin and live under fear of condemnation. Review the "in Christ" statements listed on page 75 of the text. Which of these truths is especially meaningful to you today? Choose one from each category. Write it below and consider memorizing it.

I am accepted.
I am secure.
I am significant.

When Jesus challenged His disciples to bear fruit, they were already attached to the vine (John 15:16) and therefore in a position to grow.

• According to Jesus' words in Matthew 22:37-40, what is the sum of our growth toward sanctification?

• According to 1 John 4:19 and 2 Corinthians 5:14, what enables us to love as Jesus commands us to love?

As Horatius Bonar wrote, "Reconciliation is indispensable to resemblance; personal friendship must begin a holy life."[1] Through Christ, we are friends with God (John 15:15), and we can therefore be assured that He is at work in us so that someday we will resemble His holy Son.

Father God, I am once again awed by Your love for me, and Your grace, by which You accept me as Your child. Forgive me for taking lightly my sin and for taking for granted the price You paid to change my legal and moral relationship with You. Thank You for sacrificing Your Son for my sin. Teach me to respond to that gracious gift with love for You and for others. And enable me to live out the truths that I am accepted, secure, and significant in You so that I might bear fruit for Your kingdom and, as a result of Your blessed work in my life, one day resemble Christ. I pray in His name. Amen.

A New Person
with a New Heart

Every farmer understands cause and effect. If you don't feed the sheep they die. If you don't sow seeds in the spring, there will be nothing to harvest in the fall. Let a lesson about orange trees offer a lesson about sanctification.

Ornamental orange trees are used for root stock. Once they grow to a certain height, branches are cut off and a new life (such as a navel orange) is grafted in. Everything that grows above the graft takes on the nature of the new sweet orange, and everything below the graft retains the physical characteristics of the ornamental orange.

• What does this lesson from the world of horticulture help you understand about the new birth you have in Christ?

• How should we identify ourselves as Christians according to the following passages, by the rootstock or by that which grows above the graft?
Matthew 7:20

2 Corinthians 5:16

• What grafting does Jesus teach about in John 15:1-5?

Spiritual growth in the Christian life requires a relationship with God, who is the fountain of spiritual life. Only through this relationship can we bear new seed or tap into the root of life. Unless there is a root of spiritual life within the believer, growth is impossible. There is nothing to grow.

The New Birth (78)

Since Adam and Eve, everyone who has come into this world has been born physically alive but spiritually dead (Ephesians 2:1).

Separated from God, man may look good, but—like the ornamental orange—the fruit he bears is bitter.

• According to the diagram on page 79, why is the fruit of the natural man bitter?

- What explanation for bitter fruit do you find in Jeremiah 17:9?

- What hope does the promise of Ezekiel 36:2 offer?

The moment you were grafted into the vine, you were sanctified or set apart as a child of God, and you will continue to be sanctified as He prunes you so that you may grow and bear fruit.

- Now look at the diagram on page 80. According to 1 Peter 1:3 and 23, what is the source of the new heart?

- What evidence do you see or sense in your life that, since being grafted into the vine, you are a new creation with a new life that has new desires and a new direction? Be as specific as possible. You might even ask a close friend to tell you what newness he/she has noticed in you since you named Jesus as your Savior and Lord.

As Jesus explained to Nicodemus, "you must be born again" to enter the kingdom of God (John 3:7). This new birth of the believer is also described as a regeneration (Titus 3:5). The idea in regeneration is "a new beginning."

Our Identification with Christ (81)

Another way that Scripture describes our renewal at salvation is with concepts related to Christ's death and resurrection.

Faith not only unites the believer with Christ, but also unites him with the death and resurrection of Christ (Romans 6:3,4). Turn to the list on page 82 of the text. Look up the Scripture references and explain what Paul means by identifying every believer with Christ in each of the following aspects:

In His death

In His burial

In His resurrection

In His ascension

In His life

In His power

In His inheritance

A New Man (82)

Through Christ's death and resurrection, a new creation has been effected in which all things will finally be made new. The believer who has died and now lives in Christ is part of this new creation (2 Corinthians 5:17).

• How would you refute the statement that our newness refers only to our position in Christ and that there is no real change in us until we are finally glorified?

• What do you say to explain that we still have many of the same thoughts, feelings, and experiences we had before our rebirth?

A New Master (83)

As created beings, we have no choice but to live under a spiritual power—either our heavenly Father or the god of this world. At salvation we experience a change in the power that dominates our life (Romans 6:5-7). We need to understand that this is a reality that has already taken place.

• "It is not *what* we do that determines who we are; it is *who* we are that determines what we do." What freedom does this truth offer you? What conviction and/or guidance does this statement offer for how you're living today and which master you're serving?

- In what ways, if any, are you laboring in the vineyard hoping that God will love You? In what ways are you serving with the hope that someday God will accept you?

We are neither saved nor sanctified by how we behave, but by how we believe. God already loves us, and that is why we labor in the vineyard. We already are accepted in the Beloved; that is why we serve Him.

Freedom from Sin and Death (85)

As Paul explains in Romans 6:6,7, the old self that was in bondage to sin and therefore utilized all of his bodily existence in servitude to sin and its mastery died with Christ. Now a new self exists.

- The new self is no longer under the taskmaster of sin and can now utilize his whole being as an instrument of righteousness in service to God (Romans 6:11-13). What are you doing to utilize your being as an instrument of righteousness in service to God?

Free to Live Abundantly (86)

Freedom from sin is gained through death (Romans 6:6). Sin reigns through death. But when a person dies with Christ, sin loses its mastery over that person (Romans 6:19-22). Our union with Christ in His death and resurrection means that we live spiritually and eternally in newness of life.

- In light of this truth, Paul confidently writes, "For to me, to live is Christ, and to die is gain" (Philippians 1:21).

Explain why he is able to proclaim this and why, in the way of the world (living for career, family, status, success, etc.), death is always loss.

- Why is freedom from the fear of death freedom to live the abundant life? Are you totally free from the fear of death? Why or why not?

But Why Do I Still Sin? (88)

Have you wondered, "If we are now free in Christ and we are now a new man, then why do we still sin?"
- Answer the question: "If we are now free in Christ and we are now a new man, then why do we still sin?"

- In what areas of your life are you still choosing to conform to this world? Be specific—and confess those specifics to God.

Under the dominion of God and His Son, the grace and righteousness of God dominates our lives. We can indeed know freedom from sin and death and the freedom to live abundantly.

A New Person with New Desires (90)

Identifying with Christ in His death and resurrection involves more than an external change of master. It also involves a transformation within ourselves. The newness of our person or self is seen clearly in the fact that, having been made a new creation in Christ, we have been given a new heart and, consequently, a new control center of life.

The Propensity of the Heart (91)

It is the nature of the human heart to be controlled by an outside master due to the fact that we are not the source of our life. We do not have the fountain of life in ourselves.

- Where do people in general look for life? Where have you looked or perhaps even now are looking?

- Explain why self-seeking, self-serving, self-justifying, self-glorifying, self-centered, and self-confident living is serving the god of this world.

- Besides being open to receive from the outside, the heart also becomes stamped with the character of what it takes in. When have you seen that happen to a person? Describe what happened.

- What warning is there for you personally in Jesus' words "Where your treasure is, there your heart will be also" (Matthew 6:21)? Be specific.

Desiring Change (92)

According to Scripture, the deepest desire of the believer has been changed. As Robert Jewett explains, "The heart's intentionality (or desire) is determined by the power which rules it. In the case of Christian man, the direction of the heart's intentionality is determined by Christ's Spirit."[1]

- Respond to Jewett's statement by identifying what your heart's desire is. What power is determining that desire? How is that desire different from your heart's desire before you named Jesus as Savior and Lord?

- The desire or intentionality of the human heart is its love. The identity of the believer is thus a person who, at his core, loves God rather than sin. Do you meet this criterion for a believer? Why or why not? Support your answers with specifics.

- What does genuine remorse for one's sin reveal about a person's heart and the master he or she is serving?

Our Hearts Affect Our Actions (94)

Consider now the relationship of the real core nature of the human heart to its more surface activities.

- Review J. Pedersen's ideas on pages 94-95. Give an example of a "center of action" in your life (past or present) that was formed when your soul (or heart) merged "into a new entirety."

• What insight do you gain from Pedersen that helps you explain sin in the believer's life and "good" in the life of the unbelieving sinner?

Love for God, Hatred for Sin (95)

The true nature of a person does not always express itself fully in his or her life. But the basic identity of that person is still there, and in the case of the believer, is positive toward God— as Paul's description of a believer in Romans 7:14-25 makes clear.

• Review Romans 7:14-25. What positive propensities toward God do you find in this passage?

• The believer is capable of experiencing a double servitude—servitude to the law of God and to the law of sin. At what points do you identify with Paul's struggle? Be specific.

Though at times he commits sin both in thought and act, every believer has been changed so that his deepest heart's desire is now toward God and His way. The new prevailing disposition is a love for God and a love for that which is God—that is, His Son, His people, and His righteous ways.

A Vital Understanding (99)

The believer in Christ is a new person with a new nature. Through death and resurrection with Christ, the real "inner person of the heart" has been born again. A new seed of life has been planted in the heart whose natural tendency is to grow.

- Explain why growth in the Christian life and victory over sin is impossible if a believer does not understand the reality just stated.

Not understanding who we are in Christ can truly hinder our walk with God—as the letter from one of our students illustrates (see page 100).

- Which statement(s) in the first paragraph, if any, could be your own words?

- When did you first realize the truth that "You're not a sinner, you're a saint"? (If you haven't before now will you accept that truth today?) What freedom did you experience as a result?

Again, a new seed of life has been planted in the heart of a believer, and the natural tendency of that seed is to grow. It is absolutely vital that believers understand this reality as a foundation for their spiritual growth. Otherwise, growth in the Christian life and victory over sin is impossible.

Sovereign God, thank You for the new birth that is possible because of Your grace. And thank You for the seed of new life You planted in my heart and for the innate tendency of that seed to grow. I'm understanding more about what it means to be "in Christ" and freed from sin and death. I am also aware of my responsibility to choose not to conform to my old patterns or to the ways of the world. Please give me the desire, the wisdom, and the ability to do just that as You continue to grow my Christian life. In Jesus' name. Amen.

The
COMMON
MADE
HOLY

6

Making the New Person Real

The Christian life is full of what appear to be paradoxes to the natural person. For instance, the path to glorification is death (John 12:23-26), and the path to exaltation is humiliation (Philippians 2:8,9).

Read Jesus' words to His disciples—then and now—in Matthew 16:24-26.

• What is significant about the context in which Jesus presents this paradox?

• When Jesus foretold His death and resurrection, Peter rebuked Him with, "Never, Lord!" (Matthew 16:22). Explain how this advice is essentially an encouragement to self-interest and therefore of Satan. Put more simply, explain why serving self is unwitting service to Satan.

- Returning to the paradox, what benefits—short-term as well as long-term—come with denying self?

Denying ourselves is the only way to put Christ at the center of our lives. When you deny yourself, identify with Christ, and follow Him daily, you sacrifice the pleasure of things and experience the pleasure of life.

- Why is lordship a positive rather than a negative doctrine?

- What stands at the center of your life right now? Support your answer with details about how you spend your time, your talents, and your energy.

- In what areas of your life do you need to start denying self? Be specific.

Missionary Jim Elliot said, "He is no fool who would give up what he cannot keep in order to gain what he cannot lose." Believers who know who they are in Christ understand that powerful truth.

Sin's Presence in the Believer's Life (104)

Progressive sanctification involves turning from the attitude and practice of sin with all of their negative effects in life to that of the attitude and practice of righteousness with all of their positive effects.

• In 1 John 1:7-10, John makes it clear that believers are still involved with sin: if it's necessary to continually be cleansed from sin, then we must somehow have sin. But what is the difference between "having sin" and "being sin"—and why is that difference significant?

Even though we are new persons in Christ with new dominant desires toward God and His holiness, we still sin. Sin no longer reigns over us, but it can still dwell within us.

• What does Scripture instruct us to do about that sin? See, for example, 1 John 1:9; Galatians 5:16; and 2 Corinthians 7:1.

• Look again at John Calvin's words on page 106. What "vestiges" of sin do you struggle with? How do these vestiges "humble" you? Put differently, why can—and should—our sin drive us to God before we stumble and, when we do, afterwards?

Growth in holiness means increasingly putting off the sinful desires and their actions by the increasing daily realization of our newness and the truth that we really are in Christ.

You've Already Been Changed (106)

According to Romans 6:6, our old self was crucified with Christ when we were united with Him by faith. This is a decisive and definitive act in the believer's past.

• Growth in holiness takes place when we claim the reality that we have "taken off [our] old self with its practices and have put on the new self" (Colossians 3:9,10) and act on it. What can you do—or perhaps stop doing—to "become in practice what God has already made [you]"?[1] Be specific.

• We need to renew our minds to the truth that a change has taken place in us and live accordingly by faith, with the confidence that it will work out in our experience. What truths from God's Word will help you renew your mind? Which of the verses we've looked at in these six chapters emphasize for you the fact that you have already been changed? Choose three passages to memorize and start on one today.

Accepting the tension between the past act and the present life enables us to better understand the change from the old man in Adam to the new man in Christ.

Putting on Christ (107)

Just as putting on the new man is both a past act and a present challenge, so also is the putting on of Christ a past and present matter.

- Paul speaks in the past tense in Galatians 3:27 when he says, "All of you who were baptized into Christ have clothed yourselves with Christ." What power do believers have beyond merely imitating Christ?

- After reading the commentary of James Dunn and F.F. Bruce (page 108), explain why the indicative and the imperative (the past and the present) must be balanced when it comes to putting on Christ.

In summary, we are to assume responsibility for becoming what we already are in Christ by the grace of God.

Spiritual Metamorphosis (109)

God has given us many analogies in nature to show us the wonderful transformation that salvation brings.

Consider more closely the transformation of a caterpillar into a butterfly.

- What does this analogy help you understand about your own spiritual transformation and/or how you are (or aren't) responding to its reality?

- What does the butterfly teach you about whose power is behind the transformation? What encouragement do you find in this arrangement?

- Read through the "Who Am I?" list on pages 110-111 of the text. Choose three of these statements and describe how acting on that truth would impact your life—your thoughts, your attitudes, your actions, your decisions.

The caterpillar gives up all that it is in order to become all that the Creator designed it to become. As a believer, you are to do the same.

Living Out What You Really Are (112)

The idea that Christian growth is the process of living out what happened to us at salvation is also seen in several exhortations to live according to what God has already done for us and in us.

Several passages exhort us to live a life worthy of our calling.
- What is the wording in the following passages?
Philippians 1:27

Colossians 1:10

1 Thessalonians 2:12

• Explain why being a chosen people and a royal priest-hood (1 Peter 2:9) is both a privilege and a responsibility.

• As Markus Barth points out, God equips us for our calling to be His children, which may be compared to "the bestowal of a title or a patent of nobility." [2] With what does God equip us—and what does the analogy to royalty help you understand about what God has already done for believers?

Understanding Transformation (113)

The word "transform" refers to a change in which a person's true inner condition is shown outwardly.

• How is this definition different from what you had previously understood, specifically in regards to spiritual growth?

• What do you see about transformation and this definition of it in the transfiguration of Jesus (Matthew 17:1-3; discussed on page 114)?

Dying and Rising with Christ (114)

Every Christian has died with Christ and has been raised with Him. But we have not totally realized the full reality of these events.

• Explain how Christ's death and resurrection is the pattern for what we experience in our inner person in the process of sanctification.

• What spiritual truths about sanctification are illustrated by trees frozen in the winter and seeds buried in the ground?

Just as Jesus Himself died, we have to die to who we are in Adam and give up all our dreams for self-glorification in the flesh and joyfully choose to glorify God in our bodies.

No Pain, No Gain (116)

Under the inspiration of God, Paul knew that we wouldn't fully understand all that we have in Christ. And since we don't, the problem remains that "self" will never cast out "self." We have to be led to do that by the Holy Spirit.

We often have to overcome sin even though we have already died to it.

• What does a butterfly emerging from a cocoon teach you about the value of that struggle?

- What benefits have you gained from your struggle with sin?

Our spiritual growth is connected with our endeavors to overcome sin.

- In 1 John 2:12-14, we read that "children" in the faith have overcome the penalty of sin and that the "young men" in the faith have overcome the evil one and the power of sin. What have you learned in your walk of faith about overcoming the evil one and the power of sin?

- Read again the words of John Calvin on page 117. What struggle does he describe—and what does he do when he's in that struggle?

- Let the chart on page 118 of the text serve as a mirror. What does it reveal to you about yourself?

Because of our position in Christ we are no longer "in the flesh," but since the flesh remains after salvation, we can still choose to walk according to it. We can still choose to live as a natural man, the way we did before we were born again. When we love God, we will act on that love and choose His ways instead of the ways of the flesh.

Love's Key Role in Sanctification (117)

Sanctification is nothing less than God living in us to perfect His nature in us. The fact that God is love makes love the focus of our Christian life. Knowledge of God and union with Him through Christ means a life of love.

Jesus said, "A new command I give you: Love one another. As I have loved you, so you must love one another" (John 13:34).

• Why is this a "new" command? See the discussion on page 119.

• What do you see about the kind of love you are to have for people in Jesus in Gethsemane and the words of 1 John 3:16-18?

• How does the call to love one another fit with the work of sanctification God does in His children?

Matthew 22:40 implies that the end purpose for the entire prophetic word of God is to fall in love with Him and mankind. A love for God is what ought to drive all our actions.

Look again at Henry Scougal's insightful comments on page 120. How have you been affected—both negatively and positively—by the things you have chosen to love? Be sure to include your love for Jesus.

• Love (specifically the love of God) is fundamentally what moves us. What is God's love moving you to do in the big picture as well as in the day-to-day aspects of your life? Where, if at all, are you trying to earn God's love rather than resting in it and letting it prompt your actions?

The capacity to do loving things for other people springs from the nature and character of God within us. We are not first called to do what appears to be loving things for others; we are first called to be like Christ. Loving deeds flow out of our new nature in Christ.

Love Is the Starting Point (121)

Scripture portrays love as the fulfillment of all of the commandments and righteous acts we show toward other people. Consequently, it is crucial that we focus on the character of God, which is love.

When we focus on the source of life we will bear fruit, and the fruit of the Spirit is love (Galatians 5:22).

• What relationship do you see between love and the other items listed in Galatians 5:22,23?

• Explain why love is the fulfillment of all ethical commands.

To be perfected in love is the ultimate goal of being sanctified in Christ.

- Why does the love of God compel us to love other people?

- Who has loved you with the unconditional and sacrificial love of Christ? What did you learn and/or how did you grow from that experience?

- To whom have you offered the unconditional and sacrificial love of Christ? What did you learn and/or how did you grow from that experience?

A fleshly type of love loves others because of what they do for us. It is in reality a love of self, which seeks to meet its own needs. Sanctified love, in contrast, is sacrificial and not dependent upon its object. We experience that kind of love from God, and He enables us to give that kind of love to others.

Almighty and holy God, help me to put off the sinful desires and the focus on self left over from the days before I named Your Son my Savior and Lord. Teach me to put on Christ and to live out the truth of the change You've already worked in me. And, in the words of Paul, help me to fully understand all that I have in Christ "who has blessed [me] in the heavenly realms with every spiritual blessing" (Ephesians 1:3). Enable me to overcome sin and the evil one, to resist the devil and crucify the flesh, and fill me with Your love so that I may grow to be more like Christ. Sanctify me, I pray. In Jesus' name. Amen.

The Agents of Sanctification

From germination to harvest, our sanctification is first and foremost the work of God. He is the One who drives the tractor that supplies the power, and He furnishes all the seed. He is the source of divine life that is necessary for our growth.

Scripture makes it very clear that sanctification is the work of God. At the same time, Scripture teaches the need for us to assume our responsibility for the continuing process of sanctification.
   • What encouragement do you find in the first statement?

   • What are you (the seeder in the farming analogy) doing to not get clogged?

There is a real distinction between what God has done and will do and what our responsibility is.
   • Recap the two examples given of people expecting God to do what they are responsible for (pages 127, 128).

- Where, if at all, have you looked to God to do what He has made you responsible for? How did that experience affect you and/or your walk of faith?

- Where, if at all, are you currently looking for God to do what He has made you responsible for?

When we fail to recognize the spiritual matters we are responsible for, then we set ourselves up for disappointment because we will think that either God isn't at work in our lives or that we are spiritual failures because things didn't go the way we expected.

God the Father's Role in Our Sanctification (128)

God is the primary agent of our sanctification because He is the only source of life, righteousness, holiness, love, truth, and so on. In fact, sanctification is the process of God sharing His life with and through us.

Read 2 Peter 1:3-9.
- According to this passage, what has God done to provide for our sanctification?

- And, according to this passage, what is our responsibility in the sanctification process?

- Which is more important to the sanctification process: our trying harder or our belief? Explain.

God disciplines us as part of the sanctification process.
- God doesn't punish us for doing something wrong; He disciplines us for our good in order to share in His holiness. Give one example of this from the Bible and another from your own life.

- Becoming a partaker of God's holiness does not mean we become deified. Explain the difference.

While God the Father is the primary agent, Christ and the Holy Spirit also play roles in our sanctification.

Christ's Role in Our Sanctification (131)

Jesus came that we might have life (John 10:10). At the moment of salvation, believers are joined to Christ so that He is their life.

The phrases "in Christ," "in Him," and "in the beloved" all mean that our soul is in union with God.
- Why is this union essential to our sanctification?

- What can Satan accomplish in a believer's life if that person doubts the reality of his position in Christ?

How confident are you about your position in Christ? If you're unsure, review the "I Am" list from page 75 of the text and commit to reviewing this list daily in order to increase your understanding of who you are in Christ and to build your confidence in Christ.

We could say that Christ is the mediator of God's sanctifying work.
- Explain what that statement means.

- What insight does James Dunn offer you (page 133)?

The continuing process of sanctification is a walk with God "in Christ."
- Jesus invites His people to "Come to me" and be yoked with Him (Matthew 11:28-30). What does a young ox need to learn when it is first yoked? How are you (or have you been) like a young ox?

- What message does Jesus have for you personally today in His invitation to take His yoke upon you?

When we are yoked with Jesus, we can learn to take one day at a time, to make relationships our priority, and to adopt the graceful ways of God.

The Holy Spirit's Role in Our Sanctification (135)

There do not seem to be many references in the Bible that explicitly teach that progressive sanctification is done by the Holy Spirit. Yet it's clear that Paul directly attributes the continuing process of sanctification to the Holy Spirit (1 Thessalonians 4:3-8).

• What do the following passages teach about the Spirit's connection to a believer's progressive sanctification?
    Galatians 5:22,23

    Romans 5:5

    Romans 8:4

    Romans 8:13,14

    Titus 3:5

• When praying for His followers, Jesus asks God to "sanctify them by the truth; your word is truth" (John 17:17). What is the Holy Spirit's connection to truth (John 16:13 and 14:17) and therefore our sanctification?

The work of our sanctification has all of its source in God, the Father, the Son, and the Spirit. The Father is the initiator of sanctification; Christ is the mediator whose saving work in death and resurrection provides the basis for our sanctification; and the Holy Spirit comes into all creation to sustain and enliven it. He indwells the believer to apply the sanctifying work of Christ and bring personal union with the members of the Trinity.

Our Role in Our Sanctification (136)

While it's true we are saved when we are born again and placed in Christ, we are exhorted to be actively involved in our restoration to wholeness or holiness (Philippians 2:12,13). Like Paul (Philippians 3:13,14), we are to strive for the goal or prize of our sanctification, or our conformity to Christ.

Doing Our Part (137)

When it comes to sowing and harvesting for God's kingdom, the Lord has sovereignly chosen to allow us to participate in His work.

- What does the church have in common with an electrical appliance store?

- It would be foolish to say one appliance (one believer) is better than another, for they were all designed with a different purpose in mind. What does this fact help you appreciate about the way a church is supposed to function? What is your specific role in God's church? Share your thoughts.

A Combined Effort (138)

Nothing will be accomplished to the glory of God in this present church age if we try to do everything by ourselves, if we aren't plugged into Him.

- What does Ephesians 3:10-13 teach about the combined effort God intends for us and Him? What is to result from it?

- List the commands of Romans 13:14; Romans 6:12,13; and 2 Corinthians 10:5. What would happen if believers ignored these commands?

Because God Works, We Work (139)

We are saved by faith and sanctified by faith, but faith without works is dead (James 2:14,17,18).

- What a person does is a reflection of what he or she has chosen to believe. What do your actions reveal about your belief? Put differently, what of Christ do people see in how you live?

- What does John Murray (page 140) help you understand about the relation between God's work and our work?

Explain why, even though we are called to a faith lived out in our actions, sanctification is as much a matter of faith (not works) as justification is.

What Christ Does and What We Do (140)

God works *in* us to will and to do, but He does not will and do *for* us (*see* Philippians 2:13). We must actively exercise our will and do good works.

- Explain the fact that Christ's work in salvation is substitutionary.

- Why would substitutionary sanctification not work?

The fact that sanctification is actually the restoration of true selfhood calls the human faculties of personhood (mind, emotion, and will) into action. God does not trample on our humanness; He sets us free in Christ to be fully human.

The Heart's Place in Sanctification (141)

The heart is the real person (Proverbs 27:19) and the place from which all life comes (Proverbs 4:23). The heart is thus the place of personhood, intellect, emotion, and will or actions. Sanctification is the process of changing the heart, which is actually a change of the total person.

The Heart and Our Intellect (142)

Contrary to popular thinking but according to Scripture, the heart is first the place where the human being thinks, secondly where he wills, and only thirdly where he feels. The heart is for knowing; it is the seat of reflection.

- What does Proverbs 15:14 teach about the business of the heart?

- Read each of the following passages. What mental functions are related to the heart?
  Psalm 19:14

  Psalm 90:12

Psalm 119:11

Luke 12:45

Romans 10:10

• In your own words, describe the relationship between heart and mind as it is reflected in God's Word.

The Heart and Our Will (144)

The mind represents the intellectual function of the heart. The heart is also the place where we will or purpose.

• Why can the capacity to choose be called "the greatest power we possess"?

• Why is the exercise of the will key to successful Christian living?

The Heart and Our Emotions (145)

The heart is also the place where we experience emotion, and emotions are not simply experiences of the psyche or the inner person. They are felt physically, especially in the heart.

• The Old Testament vividly expresses emotions as movements of the heart. When have you felt emotions physically? Give a specific example or two.

- When has your physical health been affected by your emotional state either positively or negatively (Proverbs 14:30 and 8:10)?

It's All in the Heart (146)

The heart is the place of knowing, willing, and feeling. It is the center of our personality. The three closely related functions of thinking, feeling, and willing all come together in the heart.

- Consequently, in the Bible, to "know" something is to grasp it such that it affects the total personality and one's behavior. What does Isaiah 1:3 show about the connection between thinking and the emotions and the will?

- Acknowledging the fact that thought, emotion, and will are united within the heart is critical to understanding Bible passages that talk about our knowledge of God and His knowledge of us. Keeping in mind that thought, emotion, and will are united within the heart, explain the teachings of the following passages.

John 17:3

John 8:32

- Knowing, feeling, and willing are seen in the concepts of hearing, purposing, and loving. Hearing, for instance, involves more than the ears. What, then, does hearing entail? In the Bible, what is the end result of purposing? What does the biblical concept of loving involve?

So often believers know the truth, but they are not living a free and productive life. That's because they do not know the truth in their hearts—they do not know it emotionally and behaviorally as well as intellectually. Likewise, hearing, purposing, and loving involves our thoughts, emotions, and actions.

Sanctification in Summary (147)

God is the primary agent of our sanctification because He gave us a new heart so that we would turn toward Him. When we do, we become an agent in our own sanctification, and our heart is conformed to the image of God.

- What lesson(s) about the heart do Henri Nouwen and his mentally handicapped friend Adam offer you?

- What encouragement have you found in this chapter's discussion about sanctification and the agents involved in the process?

As Henri Nouwen wrote, "It is our heart that is made in the image and likeness of God."[1] And it is in the heart that our mind, emotions, and will are united in Christ-centered living. When we turn our hearts toward God, we begin to love Him and others.

Almighty God and heavenly Father, I'm thankful that I'm not in this process of sanctification alone. I'm thankful that when You call me, Your child, to live a holy life, You and Your Son and Your Spirit make possible the process of my sanctification. I am aware of my role in my sanctification, and I ask You to help me to live out my faith. Continue the work You have begun. Unite my heart—my mind, will, and emotions—to know You and love You and serve You and others. I pray in Jesus' name. Amen.

Transformed by the Renewing of the Mind

In Romans 12:2, the apostle Paul writes, "Do not conform any longer to the pattern of this world, but be transformed by the renewing of your mind."

• In what areas of your life and especially your thinking are you still conforming to "the pattern of this world"?

• What recurrent or even occasional thoughts need to be replaced by God's truth and thereby renewed?

The "renewing of your mind" is crucial to our transformation and sanctification. Let's look closely at what that involves.

Reprogramming Our Minds (150)

The truth—God's truth—will indeed set us free and transform our character.

Before we came to Christ, our minds were programmed to live independent of God. In progressive sanctification, we have to assume our responsibility to reprogram our minds to the truth of God's Word.

- What resources do we have for reprogramming our minds?

  John 14:17

  John 16:13

  1 Corinthians 2:16

- What is significant about the fact that, in 2 Corinthians 10:3-5, Paul is not talking about defensive armor?

The Problem of Strongholds (152)

A stronghold is a negative pattern of thinking that has been burned into our minds either by habitual reinforcement or because of certain traumas we have experienced.

The programming of our minds is said to take place in two ways. In each category identify specific events that programmed your mind:

Prevailing early-childhood experiences

Traumatic experiences

• At the moment of salvation, there is no "clear" button to delete all the information that has been programmed into our minds. We also find ourselves confronted daily with a world system that is not godly. What messages and values of the world run counter to God's truth and His priorities for His people?

Look again at Paul's warning in Colossians 2:8 and flesh out that warning by giving several modern-day examples of the "hollow and deceptive philosophy, which depends on human tradition and the basic principles of this world."

Dealing with Temptation (153)

Even though we have the Spirit of truth to lead us, we can still choose to follow the ways of the world. Every child of God can choose to walk by the Spirit or walk by the flesh. Living in this world, we are always going to face the reality of the temptation to walk by the flesh.

• Satan knows exactly how to tempt each of us. In what areas are you particularly vulnerable?

• Why isn't shutting oneself off from the world a way to avoid temptation?

- God's way of escape from temptation is to take our thoughts captive to the obedience of Christ. What exactly does that mean—and what does it involve?

If we are going to take the way of escape from temptation which God has provided for us, we must take our thoughts captive to the obedience of Christ. If we allow tempting thoughts to ruminate in our minds, we will eventually take a path that leads to destruction.

Understanding the New Man (154)

Understanding the new man will help us understand how to take our thoughts captive to the obedience of Christ.

The Mind and the New Man (154)

To better understand how temptation affects us, we need to remember that our physical brain is part of the outer man and our mind is part of the inner man.

- Using the computer analogy, explain the relationship between the mind (the software) and the brain (the hardware). What is the function of each and how do they function together?

• What proof do you have from the Bible that problems with our thinking are due primarily to faulty software, not faulty hardware?

• We can do little to fix the hardware, but we can change the software. What does each of the following gifts from God contribute to making that change?

The mind of Christ

A new heart

The Holy Spirit

The Nervous System and the New Man (157)

The somatic nervous system regulates our muscular and skeletal movements, and we have volitional control over it. This system correlates to our will. Our autonomic nervous system relates to our glands; we have no volitional control over them, just as in a general sense we don't have volitional control over our emotions.

How Our Thoughts Affect Us

• When did you first realize that, just as your glands are regulated by your central nervous system, your emotions are a product of your thoughts; that it is not the circumstances of life that determine what we feel, but how we interpret the events of life? Give an example or two or, if this perspective on thoughts and feelings is new to you, reflect on an experience or two which helps you see its truth.

• You do have control over what you think; you can decide to believe that what God says is true. In what area(s) of your life would you do well to make that decision? In what situation, for instance, would you do well to choose to trust God rather than viewing yourself as a helpless victim of circumstance? Be specific and, to fill your thoughts with God's truth, again consider the list on page 75.

• Why is it that two people can respond differently to the same stressful situation? The major difference is software— how they mentally interpret the external world and process the data their brains receive. How does—or could—faith in God affect how you interpret and respond to the pressures of this world?

The Power of Choice

• In every tempting situation we have a choice. We can respond according to the flesh, or we can respond according to the Spirit. When has your choice to walk according to the flesh resulted in a bad habit or mental stronghold?

• What truths can a Christian suffering with an inferiority complex choose to believe?

• What thought process(es) do you need to revise in light of God's truth? Be specific.

Sanctification begins when we receive forgiveness, the life of Christ, and a new heart. It continues as we renew our minds by choosing the truth, which affects our emotions and transforms our character.

Almighty God, as I consider the challenge of transforming my mind and overcoming mental strongholds, I find great hope in the fact of Your sovereignty and love and great encouragement in the transforming truths I find in Your Word. Lord, You know the temptations I face. Enable me to believe Your truth, appropriate it by faith, and to walk by Your Spirit. I pray in Jesus' name. Amen.

The COMMON MADE HOLY

9

Truth: The Means of Sanctification

What is reality is truth, and God is the Truth and the Revealer of truth. Truth in Scripture is that which is genuine, real, and trustworthy. Anything that is opposed to God and His revelation is *un*reality or a lie.

We believe that mentally healthy people are those who have a true knowledge of God, know who they are as children of God, and have a balanced biblical worldview that includes the reality of the spiritual world.

- For a moment, let this definition of "mentally healthy" be a mirror. What do you see about yourself as you look into it?

- On which of these three points (a true knowledge of God, an accurate realization of who you are as a child of God, and a balanced biblical worldview that includes the reality of the spiritual world) could your understanding of

God's truth be stronger? How would you benefit from that clearer understanding—and what will you do to gain it?

The Trinity and Truth (163)

In the previous chapter we saw that every member of the Godhead is the source of our sanctification and life. Every one of these primary agents is also described as *true* or *truth*.

• Review the Scriptures (quoted on pages 163,164) which reveal the connection between the Trinity and truth. What do these passages reveal about the relationship between God's truth and life?

• How does each member of the Trinity make truth known to mankind?

• Explain the connection between sanctification and knowing God's truth.

The Truth Is What Changes Us (164)

Over and over Scripture teaches that we are changed or sanctified by the truth. It is the truth that brings people to God and then bears fruit in them (Colossians 1:5,6; 2 Thessalonians 2:13).

- Many commentators say that truth should be seen as the source of the righteousness and holiness that is being created in the new person. John Eadie says that "truth in Jesus has a living influence upon the heart, producing, fostering, and sustaining such rectitude and piety."[1] Give a biblical example of the power of God's truth: in the New Testament, who did Jesus influence toward a godly life? Describe that change.

- Overcoming the effects of the world, the flesh, and the devil is possible only because of our co-crucifixion with Christ. Describe each aspect of that co-crucifixion in both biblical terms (see Scripture references) and personal terms.
  Crucified to the law
  Galatians 2:19,20

  Personal experience:

  Crucified to the world
  Galatians 6:14

Personal experience:

Crucified to sin
Romans 6:6,7

Personal experience:

Crucified the flesh
Galatians 5:24,25; Romans 8:13,14

Personal experience:

Being born again involves death to self, but death is the ending of a relationship, not existence. The world, the devil, and the flesh still exist, but we have a new relationship in Christ, who has overcome all the adversaries that would keep us in bondage.

Putting Off the Old Man (167)

Renewing our mind begins with genuine repentance, and the word *repentance* means, literally, "change of mind."

In Scripture, however, *repentance* means even more: it is a change of disposition or attitude. *Repentance* implies a change that affects the whole person.

- What evidence that your repentance was genuine came when you first named Jesus your Savior and Lord? What about you—your disposition, your actions, your person—changed?

- Repentance is the first step in renewing our minds. Without repentance, the effects of the old self are still in our minds, and progressive sanctification will be stalled. Where, if at all, are you still believing the father of lies even though you are in the kingdom of light? At what points does Satan have you believing that your position in Christ isn't for real? Be specific.

The Lie Kills (168)

Believing the lie results in godlessness and wickedness, which brings the wrath of God and, finally, death. The Fall is the paradigm that the lie kills and is associated with unrighteousness.

- Adam and Eve believed the lie of Genesis 3:4 ("You will not surely die"), and the result is that mankind dies. Explain why this first sin is a real picture of all sin. What lie are we choosing to believe when we sin? Give a specific example or two. And what results from our sin?

- In John 8, Jesus shows that murder stems from the lie. Explain why lying is the root of all other sins and thus the root of murder (John 8:44).

Sin's Deceitfulness (169)

The real disease of the heart is its deceitfulness (Jeremiah 17:9).
- Describe the relationship between sin and deceit.

- When you have been tempted to sin, what lie were you tempted to believe? Be specific.

The Battle for the Mind (169)

Sin cheats man of life, which is found in truth. The real battle, then, is between Christ and the Antichrist, good and evil, the truth and the lie, divine revelation and satanic deception, the father of lies and the True One—and that battle is going on for the hearts and minds of everyone, believers and unbelievers alike.
- Mental illness, hearing "voices," and "seeing things"— explain why these may be a battle for the mind rather than a physiological problem.

- According to Ephesians 6:12, against whom are we believers struggling?

Girding Ourselves with the Truth (171)

Our first line of defense against spiritual attacks upon our minds is to gird our loins with the truth. The armor of God, like any other armor, stops penetration, yet it cannot be appropriated passively. We have to actively take our place in Christ.

- Read Ephesians 6:10-18. What armor does God provide for His people?

- What does it mean to "have girded [one's] loins with truth" (NASB)?

The only way we can overcome the father of lies is not by human reasoning, nor by scientific research, but by God's revelation—His truth.

The Word Is the Source of Truth (172)

In 2 Thessalonians 2:13, Paul writes, "From the beginning God chose you to be saved through the sanctifying work of the Spirit and through belief in the *truth*" (emphasis added). God's Word—written and incarnate in Christ—is the source of truth.

The Word Brings Life (172)

The Word of God is for us what milk is to babies. Without milk, babies don't grow, and without the Word of God, neither do we.

- What does Hebrews 4:12 teach about the Word of God and how it protects and brings life?

- What do the following passages reveal about the life-giving Word of God?
  Psalm 119 (note verses 9, 11, 16, 25, 45, 133)

Psalm 19:7

Isaiah 55:11

John 6:63

The Word Has Power (173)

If it's truth that sanctifies us, and God's Word is truth, then there is tremendous power in the Word.

- When have you experienced the life-giving power of words? Be specific.

- When have you experienced the life-giving power of God's Word? Give an example of finding strength, hope, or comfort in Scripture.

On a much smaller scale, we see in the power of human words the power of God's Word.

Finding God's Truth (174)

Sanctification takes place when we appropriate the truth. But where is the truth found?

- What of God's truth have you seen revealed in the following? Give an example or two for each.

  Through nature

  In our moral nature, even in unbelievers

  By the Spirit's presence as a witness within the heart of the believer

  Through other believers' lives

  In God's written Word

- What do you do—or could you be doing—to be aware of the truth God reveals in each of the following ways?

  Nature

Our moral nature

The conviction of the Spirit

Other believers' lives

God's written Word

Now let's look at God's written Word and why it is important to our sanctification.

The Central Truths of Sanctification (176)

Within the Bible are central truths that are essential to a believer's understanding and growth. These include truths related to our salvation and the imperatives or commands that reveal how we as Christians should live.

The beginning point of sanctification is belief in the gospel—that is, believing what God has done for us in salvation.

- Summarize in your own words what God has done for you in salvation. If you'd like, use Scripture to support your statements.

- Review what Horatius Bonar and Henry Scougal say about the relationship between faith, rest, and work (quoted on page 176). First state the connection and then comment on what you saw in a new way here.

- Consider some of the personal problems you face now or have faced in the past. What does the early church's question "Do you not know what is true of you in Christ?" help you see about those problems? How can knowing what is true of you in Christ help you address the personal problems you identified?

Growing in Truths That Apply Today (177)

We believe that God's desire for us in the ongoing process of sanctification is for us to experience in real life who we really are in Christ. This necessitates choosing on a daily basis to believe who we are as children of God.

- Read *aloud* the list of Scripture "Since I am in Christ, by the grace of God . . . " (pages 177-179). Which two or three truths are especially relevant to you today? Choose one to memorize.

Growing in Truths for the Future (180)

Making real who we are in Christ is enlivened not only by looking at the realities of the past and present in Christ, but also by exercising faith in the promises of the future.

- What do the following passages teach about that future? 1 Peter 1:3-5

2 Peter 3:13

1 John 3:2,3

- Read again the compelling words of Peter Kreeft's *Heaven: The Heart's Deepest Longing* (quoted on page 180). What realities does Kreeft identify? Why is choosing to believe those realities a powerful means of change?

Our sanctification is dependent upon believing the truth of who we are in Christ, resting in His finished work, and then living out the implications of this new perspective. As we have seen, our sanctification is also dependent on believing the truths of God's grace and the commands given to us in Scripture. Later we'll look at the place those commands have in our growth. Next, though, we'll learn how to establish the truth in our hearts by faith so we can live and walk like saints.

Almighty God, Your Word reveals that You are truth and that what You say is true no matter whether I choose to believe it or not— but I now choose to believe Your word. I also ask You to give me a new appreciation for the power of the truth as well as the power of the lie: help me to appropriate the armor You provide so I can stand strong against the lie. Also, sensitize me to the revelation of Your truth in nature, our moral nature, the conviction of the Spirit, the lives of other believers, and Your written Word—and then help me live according to it as You use it to sanctify me. Finally, help me choose on a daily basis to believe who I am as Your child. I pray in Jesus' name. Amen.

Making God's Life-Changing Truth Personal

To live a stable Christian life, we need to find the biblical balance between God's sovereignty and man's responsibility.

Balancing the sanctification teeter-totter requires some delicate maneuvering.

* What does weighting the teeter-totter toward the past-tense, positional aspects of sanctification result in?

* What does weighting the teeter-totter toward the progressive aspects of sanctification lead to?

- How in balance are you right now? Are you leaning more toward positional or progressive sanctification? Support your answer with specific evidence from your life.

At the positional end of the teeter-totter we find those who pridefully think more highly of themselves than they ought. At the opposite end are those whose professed humility is false and their "Look how humble I am" is a subtle form of pride.

- Explain what "True humility is confidence properly placed" means to a believer.

- In true humility we acknowledge our sinfulness and accept our holy God's forgiveness through the sacrificial death of Christ. Based on what you have learned so far in this study, explain how we are both saved by faith and perfected by faith in Jesus' atoning death.

If truth is the means by which we are sanctified, then faith is the means by which truth is appropriated through thought and action. In this chapter we will look at the appropriation through thought (or belief). In the next chapter, we'll examine the appropriation through action (or obedience).

Appropriating God's Truth Through Faith (185)

The writer to the Hebrews says, "Without faith it is impossible to please God" (11:6). Every aspect of life is shaped or determined by what we believe. We are saved by faith (Ephesians 2:8), and we walk or "live by faith, not by sight" (2 Corinthians 5:7). Faith is the only means by which we relate to God. The following three principles of faith need to be understood and appropriated if we hope to be led of the Lord, stay in His will, and be conformed to His image.

Faith is dependent upon its object (186)

The question is not whether you believe or how much you believe. The real question is *what* you believe or *whom* you believe in. The only difference between Christian faith and non-Christian faith is the *object* of the faith.

- According to Hebrews 13:7,8, what makes Jesus Christ the only legitimate object of our faith?

- What evidence of God's unwavering consistency—which proves He is worthy of our faith—do you see in the Bible? List five or six points and then add several points from your own life.

How much faith we have is determined by how well we know the object of our faith (187)

Our sanctification is totally dependent upon what we choose to believe. And if we choose to believe God (faith is something you decide to do), we can only have a seven-promise faith if we only know seven promises from His Word.

- Is your faith more like a seven-promise faith or a 7000-promise faith? Why—and what can you do to strengthen it?

- What is getting in the way of how well you know the object of your faith?

- Where, if at all, are you choosing to trust in one or more of God's created and fallen beings (including yourself) rather than in God?

Scripture presents faith as an action word (188)

"What good is it," James asks, "if a man claims to have faith but has no deeds?" (James 2:14).

- In common English usage, belief is mental assent or mere wishful thinking. What is the biblical meaning of belief?

- How has the "positive confession" movement twisted the concept of biblical faith or belief? How does it invite people to create their own truth?

Through prayer and reading God's Word, God reveals His truth to us. As Christians, we choose to believe the truth; we don't choose what truth is. Truth originates in heaven, and our responsibility is to believe it.

Storing the Truth in Our Hearts (190)

The faith that will actually change our character and consequently our behavior involves appropriating the truth in our hearts so that our faith is not just mental assent.

In Colossians 3:15 and 16, we learn that the truth that centers on Christ—which He embodies—is to be at the very core of our being. We are to let His peace arbitrate the matters of our heart. Arbitration is necessary because the voices of the world, the flesh, and the devil are contending for control.

- What voices of the world, the flesh, and the devil are especially persistent in your life these days? Be specific.

- What does God's truth say to these voices? What arbitration does it offer? Again, be specific.

Remember the pitcher that was contaminated with coffee over the years (page 191)?

- What made the pitcher clean eventually?

- What can make your mind and heart clean?

- What are you doing—or could you be doing—daily to renew your mind?

God has revealed Himself and His ways in His Word, and it is our responsibility to know the truth that is revealed there. According to Scripture, meditation is a sure way to let the Word of God richly dwell within us (2 Timothy 2:15).

Meditation and Holiness (192)

Let's see what we can learn about the discipline of meditation in biblical history.

The Great Value of Meditation (192)

According to Joshua 1:8, meditating on God's Word is the key to successful or, better, wise living.
- Living wisely involves doing according to the truth of the Word of God. How can meditation help you do that?

- Read Psalm 1:1-3. What do you see here of the value of meditating on God's Word?

Meditation in the Bible (193)

The concept of meditation is mentioned throughout the Bible.
- Look again at Deuteronomy 6:6-9. What will result from meditating on God's Word? What evidence of this have you seen in a Christian you know?

- What sustained David when he was fleeing for his life? When have you drawn strength and comfort from God's Word in depressing or oppressive circumstances?

- What three steps—based on what David did—could you try the next time you can't sleep at night?

The Meaning of Meditation (194)

Meditating on God's Word helps us go beyond superficial obedience to His commands. It helps us absorb the rich meaning of what He has to say.
- What did you learn about the meaning of meditation from the discussion of the Hebrew words *haghah* and *siach*?

- Choose a favorite or familiar verse from Scripture and meditate on it as we meditated on Psalm 23:1. What new insight did you gain or what truth did you come to appreciate more?

Wrong Uses of Meditation (196)

The object of our meditation—just like the object of our faith—is the critical issue.

- What did you learn about the right uses of meditation from this discussion of wrong uses of meditation?

- When, if at all, have you participated in the wrong use of meditation—in guided imagery, directing your thoughts inwardly, attempts to induce a passive state of mind? What will you do to overcome any possible damage done by these activities?

How Meditation Can Change Us (198)

Thinking wrong thoughts can lead to despair—as David and Jeremiah experienced. But they also knew the power of choice: they chose to believe in God's unfailing love, salvation, goodness, compassion, and faithfulness even when the hard circumstances didn't change.

• When, in the midst of difficult times, have you deliberately chosen to believe the truth about God—His unfailing love, salvation, goodness, compassion, and faithfulness—despite circumstances which suggested the contrary? What change did that meditation work in you, if only for a little while?

• In Philippians 4:7,8, Paul calls us to focus on whatever is true, noble, right, pure, lovely, admirable, excellent, and praiseworthy. What are you doing to think scripturally about all aspects of life?

How Meditation Can Affect Our Actions (200)

Whatever we meditate on in our minds goes into our hearts and affects our actions.

• Meditation is a lot like learning to ride a bike or drive a car. Just as those actions become almost unconscious, so when we continually think on God's Word, it enters the depth of our hearts. When, if ever, has God's truth guided you almost unconsciously? Describe the situation.

• Meditating on God's Word is simply talking to our hearts so that the Word of God is instilled there and comes out in our actions. What statements of biblical truth (or soliloquies) would be helpful if they became part of your conversation with your heart? List three or four points and choose one to start focusing on.

The Objects of Our Meditation (201)

The first object of our thoughts should be God Himself—to worship Him, to ascribe to Him His divine attributes. Beyond God and His ways, we should meditate on whatever is good (Philippians 4:8).

• Rather than denying negative circumstances, we can face those problems and address them with God's truth (see page 202 for examples). Below, list any negative circumstances you're facing. Next to each write out a statement of God's truth that you can dwell on in the midst of those circumstances.

• Is there a place for sanctified imagination? Is there such a thing as Christian visualization? Explain your answer.

Truth, Christ, and Ourselves (203)

Jesus was the embodiment of the written Word, the personification of truth. If we were fully sanctified in the truth, we would think, feel, and do what Jesus did.

• Explain why it is less than Christian for us to say we know the Word of God when it has not touched our hearts nor transformed our character to Christlikeness.

• When truth is appropriated, it touches every aspect of the heart. We are emotionally transformed and our wills are moved to action. Describe a time when you have experienced this truth (what emotions and actions resulted?) or identify a current situation in which appropriating God's truth would transform you emotionally and move you to action.

Thinking Upon the Truth (204)

We stated earlier that our emotions are the product of our thought life. We are not shaped so much by the external events in life as we are by how we perceive them. If what we think does not reflect truth, then what we feel does not reflect reality.

• Remember the hypothetical job interview? When have your false thoughts caused feelings that did not reflect reality?

• How have Satan's lies held you back in your Christian walk—or how might they be doing so? We invite you to work through the Steps to Freedom in Christ so that you can experience an intimate relationship with your heavenly Father.[1]

The Place of Emotions (206)

The coming together of thought, feeling, and action in the heart can be seen in the life of Christ.

- What did compassion move Christ to do? What did anger compel Jesus to do?

- When has sorrow led you to repentance? What actions resulted from this feeling of sorrow and regret you had after sinning? Explain how thought, feeling, and action converged for you.

Meditation Increases Our Faith (209)

When we meditate on God's greatness and His love for us, and when we see all that He has done for us, we are led to place our confidence—our faith—in Him.

- What has God done to confirm His love for you in the past? Be specific. When have you clung to the truth of that love and not let circumstances erase it? Again, be specific.

- When we realize that God is always present and at work in our lives, life becomes different. Have you realized that fact? If so, how is life different now? If not, how would life be different—and what's keeping you from choosing to believe the truth that God is in fact always present and at work in your life?

Practical Methods of Meditation (210)

Meditation is basically thinking on the Word of God, going over its truth in our minds repeatedly so that God's truth finally reaches our hearts, affecting our emotions and will. The following process may help you hide God's Word in your heart.

• Briefly define in your own words what each step involves and why it is important.

1. *Personalize the truth (210).*

2. *Visualize the truth (211).*

3. *Respond to the truth (211).*

4. *Let God's Word transform you (212).*

5. *Meditate on the Word to strengthen your relationship with the Author (212).*

• Now choose a passage and, focusing on that truth, walk through the five steps. Note how you personalized it, what you visualized, how you responded, and/or how it strengthened your relationship with God.

It is a fundamental truth of Scripture that we as Christians live by the Word of God. We are born again by the Word, and we grow by the Word. The Word is the food of our soul.

- Why is this analogy a strong argument for daily meditation on God's Word?

- What did psychologist Paul Meier's study of the power of meditation reveal? What is God's message or call to you in that study and this chapter on meditation?

Consider again these words from Horatius Bonar: "He that would be like Christ, moreover, must study him . . . He that would be holy must steep himself in the word, must bask in the sunshine which radiates from each page of revelation . . . Exposing ourselves constantly to this light, we become more thoroughly 'children of light.'"[2]

Lord God, in this chapter I was reminded that the "Faith Hall of Fame" members had great faith because they had a great God—and so do I, and I praise You for Your greatness. Clearly, meditation on Your Word will result in a sharpened awareness and a better appreciation of Your greatness. Keep me faithful in this daily infusion of truth and enable me to store what I learn in my mind that I may stand strong in You, whatever the circumstances of my life, and so that You may continue to conform me to the image of Christ. I pray in His precious and powerful name. Amen.

The Power of Our Actions

As we have said, truth is the means by which we are sanctified, and faith is the means by which truth is appropriated through thought and action. Having looked at appropriating truth through thought (or belief), we will now examine appropriation through action (or obedience).

Understanding Christian Growth (215)

The apostle Paul sets forth the cycle of Christian growth in Colossians 1:9-12.

As you look at that cycle as it is diagrammed on page 216, complete the chart below by answering what prompts growth at each point and what we can do to block growth at each point.

To Experience Growth . . .   To Block Growth . . .

Stage 1

Stage 2

To Experience Growth...   To Block Growth...

Stage 3

Stage 4

• Which stage of Christian growth do you find most difficult? What are you doing either to experience growth in
your faith or to block that growth?

• When I (Neil) took seriously the truth that I was
working for God at the company where I was an engineer,
that truth transformed me. When has God's truth taken
hold of your heart and transformed you—by, for instance,
changing your perspective, convicting you of sin, calling
you to love someone, or commanding you to share your
faith?

Christian growth happens when we choose to live according to
what we understand. When we do so—when we exercise our
will by being submissive through humble obedience to God—

we grow in the knowledge of God. In other words, we receive greater knowledge as we act on the knowledge we already have.[1]

The Paths to Change (219)

In previous chapters we learned that changing the heart begins with a change of thought or belief. When truth penetrates the heart, it touches our emotional core, which motivates us to action. Now let's consider how our actions influence both our thoughts and emotions.

Our Actions Can Affect Our Feelings (219)

We don't always feel our way into good behavior; rather, we behave our way into good feeling. Our behavior can indeed change how we feel.
• Read Psalm 13. What does David show us here about changing our feelings by changing our behavior?

• Scripture commands us to rejoice and be joyful, to show love, have peace, and not give in to fear. Keeping in mind that our behavior can change how we feel, what could you do the next time you're feeling these feelings?
Sad rather than joyful

Unloving rather than loving

Anxious rather than peaceful

Fearful rather than confident

In Scripture, emotion was not simply an inner feeling; it was re-lated to action. And the fact that emotions are commanded and often obligatory—as in the case of joy—suggests that the rela-tionship was not always from feeling to action. It could also go from the action to the feeling.

Our Actions Can Affect Our Thoughts (224)

Just as actions can affect our emotions, our actions can affect our thoughts and beliefs. Our actions not only reflect the thoughts and emotions of our hearts; they also shape our hearts.

- The woman's decision to live as though there was a God helped her become a Christian. When have your actions af-fected your thoughts or beliefs? Give an example.

A Principle Affirmed in Scripture (225)

- In the Bible knowing involves action; faith involves obe-dience; and wisdom involves practical skills for living life. How are these understandings different from our Western outlook?

A Principle Taught in Scripture (226)

- In 1 John 3:16-18, for instance, Scripture teaches that actions can affect our thoughts. What actions are commanded here? What thoughts will follow if we act obediently?

- When have your experiential actions of love led you to the real knowledge of love?

The Need to Be Willing (229)

- You probably won't understand the will of God if you are not willing to do it. If you are willing to do His will, then you will likely know what it is. When has taking a step of faith (acting) led to clearer understanding (thoughts) about what God is doing?

In the heart, thought and action are inseparably tied together. You cannot affect one without having an effect on the other. Not only does a thought lead to action, but the action also strengthens the thought behind it.

Our Actions Can Affect Our Knowledge (231)

When the Bible talks about how our actions affect our thoughts, we find that there is an interesting interplay between knowledge and action.

- What person in the Bible gained knowledge of God by acting? Give an example. You might consider Abraham (being willing to sacrifice Isaac), Peter (obediently going to Cornelius to share the gospel), or Ruth (loyally acting to serve Naomi).

- When have you gained knowledge of life or the Lord by an action you took? Give an example, perhaps using a lesson learned from a mistake.

Psalm 111:10 says, "The fear of the Lord is the beginning of wisdom; a good understanding have all those who do His commandments" (NASB). Actions can indeed affect our knowledge.

Our Actions Can Affect Our Faith (231)

Scripture clearly teaches that faith and works are related, and James says that the flow goes both ways. Faith produces works, but works also affect faith.

- Give a biblical example of a person whose faith in God was affected by his or her actions. You might consider, for instance, Jonah (running from God), Peter (denying Christ as He had predicted), or the woman who reached out to touch Jesus' clothes and was healed.

• When have your actions affected your faith in God? Give an example of perhaps stepping out boldly for the Lord and seeing Him be faithful to you.

Just as our actions can affect our feelings, our thoughts, and our knowledge, our actions may also add new dimensions to our understanding of God and His work or simply strengthen the understanding we already have.

Showing Ourselves Faithful (232)

Growing in the Christian life involves both right belief about life and the knowledge that comes only through the practice of living that life.

A wise saint wrote that "it is one of life's great compensations that you cannot sincerely help another without helping yourself in the process."

• When have you found this statement to be true?

• What does this statement suggest about how we can "show ourselves faithful"?

Our duty as God's children, saved by the death of His Son, is to do what clearly lies at hand.

- According to Matthew 22:37-40, what are the two greatest commandments in the Law?

- How can you love God "with all your heart and with all your soul and with all your mind" (verse 37)?

- What can you do to "love your neighbor as yourself" (verse 39)? Consider those people closest to you by marriage, by blood, and by proximity.

Having biblical knowledge by itself does not necessarily change our life, but when we practice God's truth and love Him and our neighbors as He calls us to, we gain in our knowledge and insight into His truth. A change of heart includes both change of mind and change of action.

Lord God, thank You for Your plan of sanctification, Your plan to make me more like Your Son. Please show me where I'm blocking growth in that direction and what I need to do to help that growth happen. I've realized that my actions are key to that growth, so I ask You to, when I'm feeling unloving or down, give me the strength to choose to act lovingly, trusting that feelings will follow. And, realizing how my actions can affect my feelings, my thoughts, my knowledge, and my faith in You, I ask You to help me act in ways that please You. Show me Your ways of love—I am willing to follow—and enable me to walk according to them. I pray in Jesus' name. Amen.

The COMMON MADE HOLY

12

Does God's Law Apply Today?

The two extremes of legalism and license sit on opposite ends of a teeter-totter.

Legalism and license are in delicate balance within the concept of freedom.

• What can weighting the teeter-totter toward "You are free in Christ! Don't go back to the law" result in?

• What can weighting the teeter-totter toward denial that there is such a thing as freedom from sin and the past lead to?

• How in balance are you right now? Are you leaning more toward license or legalism? Support your answer with specific evidence from your life.

Our freedom in Christ is the fulcrum for the legalism/license teeter-totter.

Living Free in Christ (236)

Christians are indeed positionally free in Christ, but how many are living like they are? If a person isn't experiencing freedom in Christ, then he is stymied in his growth.

When people are alive and free in Christ, they know who they are in Christ, bear fruit, and have a satisfying prayer and devotional life. When problems arise, they resolve them in Christ. Using these criteria, evaluate to what degree you are free in Christ.

- Read through the undergraduate's letter to Neil. What, if anything, about her "before" experience is similar to what you deal with? What does your answer suggest about how free you are in Christ? Again, to what degree are you living free in Him?

When people have their eyes opened to the truth about who they are in Christ and have resolved their personal and spiritual conflicts, watch them grow!

Making the Right Choice (238)

Sin should not be our master (Romans 6:14), but we can choose to live as though we are still under the law and thereby rob ourselves of the freedom Christ purchased for us on the cross. We can also go to the other extreme. Both legalism and license lead to bondage that can be resolved only through repentance and faith in God.

- How is license like jumping off a cliff? Discuss the initial sense of freedom and the consequences of that choice.

- How is legalism like a forest fire? What message does the accuser have for those who choose legalism?

Temptation and accusation are two sides of the same coin that Satan flips in his relentless pursuit of our defeat. We are truly liberated in Christ when we walk the tightrope between legalism and license.

The Curse of Legalism (239)

The Bible's teaching is clear: "No one is justified before God by the law, because, 'The righteous will live by faith'" (Galatians 3:11). So why are we still struggling with legalism after 2,000 years of church history?

- It's not God's law that is a curse, but legalism. Explain the difference.

- The law is powerless to give life (Galatians 3:21). Telling someone that what he is doing is wrong does not give him the power to stop doing it. When have you experienced that truth for yourself?

- The law actually has the capacity to stimulate our desire to do what it prohibits. When have you experienced that power or seen it affect someone else, perhaps a child?

Thankfully we are not saved by how we behave, but by how we believe, or nobody would have any hope.

What *Is* God's Law? (240)

Now that we are in Christ and no longer under the law, how do we relate to the law? To answer that, we need first to understand what the law of God is.

Review the discussion on pages 240-242 and list all that the word "law" can refer to.

- What item(s) on the list surprised you?

- In light of your list, explain why to encounter God's law is to come in contact with God.

God's commands are an expression of His love for us (they are protective rather than restrictive) and the sum of what it means for us to live in love toward God and our neighbor.

- What do God's commands show you about His love for you?

- Peter Craige writes that the commandments "provide the framework within which the Israelites could express their love of God . . . the people were to think on them and meditate about them, so that obedience would not be a

matter of formal legalism, but a response based upon understanding."[1] Is your obedience to God's law an expression of
your love for Him? Why or why not? Is your obedience "a
matter of formal legalism" or "a response based upon understanding"? Explain.

God's laws are nothing less than the moral law of the universe
that rightly relates and binds man to God and his fellow man in
the perfect way of truth and life. His laws, then, are an essential
aspect of the truth that we must focus on to know a transformed
life.

Our Relationship to God's Law (243)

The person without Christ stands before the law as a sinner and
lawbreaker. He lives under the condemnation of the law and
the penalty of death. But the believer "in Christ" has the same
relationship to the law that Christ has.

We Are Free (244)

And what is Christ's relationship to the law? Christ is the fulfillment or goal of the law: the total significance of law has been
attained in him.

  • The law was the instrument of the just condemnation of
  lawbreakers. How did Christ fulfill that aspect of the law?
  See Galatians 3:13.

• The law was the expression of God's will. How did Christ fulfill this aspect of the law? See Matthew 26:36-42; John 6:38; and Philippians 2:8.

Free from Legal Bondage (245)

• Under the law, violators of the law are rightly deserving of punishment. Explain how "in Christ" we are free from that legal bondage. See Romans 6:5; Romans 7:6; Romans 8:1,2; 1 Corinthians 1:30; and Galatians 3:13.

Free from the Legal Requirement (245)

• The law served as a "supervisory custodian" for God's people in Old Testament times. Describe the role of a custodian and then explain how, in Christ, we no longer need such a tutor. Use the analogy of your relationship today to the rules your parents had when you were growing up.

• In the time before Christ, the law was not a way to earn God's grace or become His people. In the law, God was simply asking His people to live in accordance with the principle of righteousness that would bring to them the experience of the promised blessing. Who was not able—and who was able—to fulfill this contract? Explain how a believer in Christ has fulfilled the contract.

Being in Christ, the believer does not strive to meet the righteous demands of the law. Rather, the believer strives to allow Christ's righteousness—which has already met all of the law's demands—to be worked out in his life so that he might be conformed to the image of His Savior.

We Are Responsible (249)

The grace of God makes us free to be what we were created to be—free to do what we know in our hearts that we should do. This kind of freedom is known only in relation to God, and that cannot exclude His righteous law.

• Explain how sanctification and growth in holiness is, in reality, growth in conformity with God's laws.

• Why does living in Christ as the fulfillment of the law call for careful study of the entire Bible? In answering, consider all that Christ fulfilled as well as the truth of 2 Timothy 3:16,17.

As Christians, we are free from the law and yet obligated to keep the commandments of the "law of Christ." Lawkeeping is the result of a relationship with Christ, not the means to gain such a relationship. Finally, sanctification is working out the righteousness that is ours because of who we are in Christ.

A Divine Empowerment (252)

We cannot sanctify ourselves by keeping the law. Sanctification is applying the finished work of Christ in our lives through the power of the Holy Spirit. Put differently, the power to live according to Christ's law comes only through the Spirit as He lives Christ's life (which was victorious over all sin) in and through us.

An Obedience Compelled by Love (253)

Motivating God's people by fear or laying down the law without grace is a blatant denial of the Gospel. God's perfect love casts out fear (1 John 4:18).

- When has love for an authority figure compelled you to obey him or her? Compare such obedience prompted by love to obedience motivated by fear. Which is easier? Why?

- What is there about the Cross that compels you to obedience?

He First Loved Us (254)

Love has its source only in God (1 Timothy 1:14), and it is God's love that enables the believer to love (1 John 4:19).

- When has God clearly enabled you to love someone? Consider, for instance, a time you offered forgiveness or an act of kindness.

- What did that experience teach you about God's love?

As Paul said, "The entire law is summed up in a single command: 'love your neighbor as yourself'" (Galatians 5:14)—and, to answer the chapter title's question, yes, that law applies today.

The Benefits of God's Law (255)

The commands of the law of Christ are part of the truth that God uses to transform our lives and bring increasing sanctification or holiness.

- Why has God given us His moral laws?

- Explain how God's commands are aspects of truth designed to help us have true freedom and joy.

We must never look at God's commands as restrictions on our freedom and joy, but as aspects of truth designed to help us have true freedom and joy.

Almighty God, I thank You for what I've realized about Your law and I thank You that Christ has already met all of the law's demands. I ask that You would enable me to allow Christ's righteousness to be worked out in my life so that I might be conformed to the image of my Savior and filled with His love. I ask You, Holy Spirit, to enable me to live according to Christ's law as You live in and through me. I pray in Jesus' name. Amen.

Abiding in Christ:
The Source of Holiness

Christian maturity is Christlike character. It's not knowing the principles or trying hard to live the Christian life. Only by God's grace can we live the Christian life. Only God can redeem us from the power of sin, set us free from our past, and make us new creations "in Christ."

Christ's Strength or Yours? (258)

When we become Christians, we are inwardly connected to the only source of power that is able to overcome the laws of sin and death, and that source is the law of the Spirit of life in Christ Jesus (Romans 8:2). One of the greatest temptations we face is to stop being dependent on God, our source of power, and instead rely on our own intellect and resources to live the Christian life.

• What does Luke 2:52 teach us about true Christian growth?

- What aspects of your life need to be in balance for true Christian growth?

- What does the diagram on page 259 show about why you fail in your attempt to be disciplined in the aspects of life you just listed?

The further we are from the hub, the harder we try to fulfill the Bible's commands in our own strength.

- What needs to be at the hub of the wheel? And what does it mean to be plugged in to the hub?

- Read again the paragraph starting on page 259 to determine how close you are to the hub: where in that description do you see yourself?

Parachurch ministries, radio programs, and countless books are part of a concerted effort to save the family in America—but families haven't gotten any stronger, and our children don't seem to be doing any better. Again, what's wrong has to do with how far away from the hub we are.

Where Changed Behavior Begins (261)

We cannot approach the Christian life merely by looking at the Bible's practical applications. We need the necessary foundation:

being established in Christ. Only when we understand who we are in Christ and how to live by the Spirit's power can we begin to apply the practical applications we find in God's Word.

People who try to behave as children of God will produce little fruit when they have no understanding of who they are in Christ or how to live by the Spirit's power.

- Why do I (Neil) tell many couples struggling with their marriage to temporarily stop trying to fix it?

- Read Proverbs 23:7. What support for my approach does this verse offer?

Before people can change, they must first become established in their freedom in Christ so they know who they are as children of God.

- Read John 15:4-7. What is the context of the call to "bear much fruit"—and what is significant about that context?

- What fruit for the kingdom are you bearing in your life today? If you're not sure, ask your spouse or a close friend to help you answer the question.

• What does your answer suggest about to what degree you are abiding in Christ and to what degree you are trying to live the Christian life in your own strength?

No matter how long you are a Christian, your need to remain dependent on Christ stays constant. Only with Him at the center of your life can you bear fruit.

• Is Christ at the center of your life? Your marriage? Your home? Your ministry? (Every believer has a ministry.) Explain the basis for your answers.

• Put differently, are you living more according to a law principle (are you trying to obey?) or the principle of grace (are you walking by faith according to what God said is true and living by the power of the Holy Spirit?)? Again, explain the basis for your answers.

Someone once said that if the Holy Spirit were taken away from us, 95 percent of what we do in our churches would still go on as scheduled. The same may be true of your marriage, your family, and your ministry.

God, Our Power Source (264)

Scripture repeatedly teaches that sanctification in our daily lives is possible only through the power of God. We are to abide in Christ, for without Him we can do nothing (John 15:4-7). But what does it mean to "abide in Christ" or "walk by faith" in the "power of the Holy Spirit" so that true growth in holiness takes place?

The Trinity's Involvement (264)

In Scripture we see that Christ, the Spirit, and the Father are all involved in our daily growth. Let's examine the roles that each member of the Trinity has in our growth.

In Our Salvation (264)

- According to Titus 3:4-6 and Romans 8:2-4, what is the activity of the Father in our salvation? The role of the Son? The role of the Holy Spirit?

In Our Sanctification (265)

- What is the role of the Father in our sanctification? The role of the Son? And the role of the Holy Spirit?

What Christ Does, the Spirit Does (265)

Scripture frequently mentions that Christ and the Spirit have identical places in the world of salvation, especially in relation to our sanctification. The Spirit comes to bring into our lives the presence of the risen Lord and all that He is.

• Review the parallel "job descriptions" of Jesus and the Spirit on page 265. Summarize their work in your salvation and comment on what is significant about their identical roles.

• In Revelation 2 and 3, each of Christ's letters to the churches closes with "He who has an ear, let him hear what the Spirit says to the churches" (Revelation 2:7,11,17,29; 3:6,13,22). What keeps you personally—and the church today in general—from listening to and hearing the Spirit?

• What does Ephesians 3:14-17 help you see about the relationship between the Spirit and Christ in the Christian life? See also John 16:14 and 1 Corinthians 12:3.

The basic principle of our growth is to remain focused on Christ our Savior through every means by which He is revealed and to do so in openness to the Spirit of God, who works in us to make Christ's victorious life dynamic in our lives.

Abiding in Christ (267)

The Bible clearly teaches that our life, strength, and all our activities as believers are to be related to Christ. They are to flow out of our being in union with Christ.

This truth could not be made clearer than it is in Jesus' statement about the necessity of abiding in Him (John 15:4,5).

• Considering all you've read so far, why does it make sense that we must abide (remain or continue) in Christ if we are to bear fruit?

• What do you learn about abiding in Christ from His relationship with His Father? Comment on the fact that, in both instances, the abiding is mutual.

• As a result of abiding in His Father, what did Christ's life reveal? What, then, will your life (your words, your actions, your thoughts) exhibit as you abide in Christ?

The Practice of Abiding in Christ (268)

Scripture teaches that abiding in Christ involves nourishing ourselves through faith in Christ and following Him by obeying His commands.

Receiving Christ by Faith (269)

• We first receive by faith all that Christ is for us (in Him we are rightly related to God as His beloved children), and then we abide in Him by letting His words abide in us (John 15:7). What are you doing to let the words of Jesus abide in you? What could you be doing to let His truths help you more fully come to know and treasure Him as your personal Truth and Life?

Obeying Christ's Commands (269)

• Like Jesus, for us to abide in Christ means that we live in obedience to our Lord's commands (John 15:9,10). This means showing the same kind of love He showed. What can you do today to show Christ's love to someone?

Living in union with Christ, which is essential for growth in holiness, involves both our constant receiving of supernatural life from the vine and a determination to follow Christ in our daily walk. Evaluate how constantly you're receiving the supernatural life and how determined you are to follow Christ moment by moment.

The Priority of Abiding in Christ (270)

When we read about fruit-bearing in John 15, we subtly hear and focus on an imperative to bear fruit.

• What must happen before we can bear fruit?

- What must happen before we can love one another?

Conforming to the image of God is a long, steady process of internal change as we abide in Christ, as we are yoked to Jesus (Matthew 11:29).

The End Result (271)

Read again the poem entitled "The Wreath."
- How is your life—or how has your life been—like that "rustic wreath"?

- Who in your life has God used to "gently shape His wreath"?

We grow as believers by focusing on Christ and abiding in Him by faith so that His life is lived in us. We lay hold of Him as our total salvation—past, present, and future. He not only rescued us from sin and death, but He continues to save us, conforming us to His righteousness as we follow His pattern of life in obedience to His will.

Almighty God, it is indeed a very real temptation for me to stop being dependent on You and instead rely on my own intellect and resources to live the Christian life. Please continue to teach me how to live by the Spirit's power, how to abide in You, and how to walk by faith so that I can grow in holiness. Put simply, please continue to teach me to trust and obey. I thank You, God, for the gift of Your Son and the provision of Your Spirit so that I can indeed be sanctified and bear fruit for Your kingdom. In Jesus' name. Amen.

Filled with the Spirit:
The Power of Holiness

We who name Jesus as Lord and Savior are to focus on Christ, and live by the dynamic of the Spirit. Christian growth is accomplished only by the Spirit, and it is absolutely necessary for us to be rightly related to Him and sensitive to His leading.

- Look again at the account of the young pilot's flight through the fog. At what points of this analogy to a believer being guided by the Spirit did you realize something about God's Spirit? About yourself? About your relationship to the Spirit?

- Every aspect of our Christian life is performed by the Spirit. Consider the list on page 275 and then identify any areas where you are trying to manage on your own, apart from the Spirit.

Scripture gives us four commands about our relationship with
the Spirit. Two are positive: "walk by the Spirit" (Galatians 5:16
NASB); "be filled with the Spirit" (Ephesians 5:18). And two are
negative: "do not grieve the Holy Spirit" (Ephesians 4:30); "do
not quench the Spirit" (1 Thessalonians 5:19). These commands tell us how we can enjoy a right relationship with the
Spirit.

Walking by the Spirit (275)

The Greek word translated "walk" literally means "to go about,
to walk around." How a person lives or conducts his life is con-
sidered to be the way he walks.

- According to Scripture, a godly person walks as if he
were always before God. What about your day so far would
have been different if you had been conscious that you were
in fact before God?

- What would you say is the source of power in your life
and the direction of your life?

- What would walking by the Spirit (or walking more by
the Spirit) mean for your life—for the power by which you
are living and for the direction you are headed?

Inhibiting the Work of the Spirit (277)

When we sin, we hinder our fellowship with the Spirit and grieve Him. Sin is not only the breaking of God's law; it is also the wounding of His heart. Furthermore, we quench the Spirit's ministry by refusing to heed His direction or rejecting His ministry from others.

- What are you doing that is hindering your fellowship with the Spirit? Confess that sin and turn from it.

- In what areas of your life, if any, are you refusing to heed the Spirit's direction or rejecting His ministry from others?

- Walking by the Spirit requires that we be sensitive to sin in our lives. What specifics in each of the following categories do you need to confess? Also list areas where you are vulnerable.

  Wrong actions

  Selfish desires

  Fleshly thoughts

- Walking by the Spirit also means renouncing all forms of worldliness. What specifics in each of the following categories do you need to renounce? Again, also list points where you are vulnerable.

Human wisdom

Human standards

Human righteousness

Summarize what a believer—what you—need to do about the sin you have identified. Let 1 John 1:9 guide your answer.

Being Filled with the Spirit (279)

Obeying the negative commands that call us to avoid hindering the Spirit's ministry is vital for walking or living by the Spirit. But equally, if not more, important is Paul's positive command "Be filled with the Spirit" (Ephesians 5:18).

The Meaning of Being Filled (279)

- To be filled with the Spirit means to let the Spirit who lives in us manifest Himself so that His presence fills us and controls all of our thoughts and actions. What of your own self-interests and self-sufficient ways do you need to empty yourself of so you can be filled?

• When have you set your mind on something? What was the result of your focus or preoccupation? What does that situation suggest about what it means to set your mind on the things of the Spirit (Colossians 3:2)?

The Means to Being Filled (280)

• If we want to be filled with the Spirit, then we must be people of prayer, students of the Word, and active in the church. Why is each of these elements a means of being filled by the Spirit?

Prayer

The Word

The corporate body of believers.

• Are you letting yourself be filled with God's Spirit? Evaluate your prayer life, your Bible study, and your fellowship. Note what will you do to improve in each category and which step toward that end you will take this week.

Prayer

The Word

The corporate body of believers.

The Yearning to Be Filled (281)

- If we want to be filled with the Spirit, we must have a genuine desire to live a holy life. When have you been really thirsty? What did you do to work up that thirst?

- What can you do to develop a thirst for the Holy Spirit?

The Holy Spirit will guide you out of darkness and into the light, where you can enjoy fellowship with God and other believers. He is first and foremost the Spirit of truth, and He will lead us into all truth. Our responsibility is to respond to that truth by faith.

Faith Is Where it All Begins (282)

The process of salvation, from beginning to end, is a matter of living by faith. Growth in sanctification, therefore, may be summed up as growing in the exercise of faith.

Faith Calls for Our Participation (283)

Faith is simply responding to God, to what He does and says. When we hear God tell us something and we respond, we are exercising faith. Living by faith means acting in faith.

- John White says, "Do not look inside yourself and ask, 'How much faith do I have?' Look to God and ask, 'What is he saying to me? What would he have me do?' "[1] What is encouraging about this way of looking at faith?

• So what is God saying to you today—and how will you respond? And what would God have you do today—and when will you do it?

• What does the account of Jesus healing the man's shriveled hand (Mark 3:1-6) show you about faith needing to be active?

• Read Philippians 2:12,13. What connection between our activity in faith and God's enabling power do you find there? Hint: It is your responsibility to have faith, hope, and love, yet all of these are gifts of God.

• Living by faith means obeying God's commands even when they seem contrary to reason. When have you taken such a step—or where could you today? Consider overcoming a sin habit or making a major decision, something which calls for you to depend fully on the power of Christ's life in you.

Faith Calls for Total Dependence (284)

It is by faith that we live and grow in holiness. God has provided a perfect salvation from beginning to end. Faith believes this reality and acts on the basis of it (see 2 Peter 1:3-5).

• How is exercising our faith different from exercising our willpower? What does exercising our faith do that merely exercising our willpower can't accomplish? What is the role of grace in our exercise of faith?

• Explain "the activity of faith is not *for* life, but *from* life."[2] Again, what is the role of grace in "the activity of faith"?

Becoming What We Will Be (285)

C.S. Lewis observed that faith causes us to "pretend" to be what we are not yet.[3]

• Think of a person in the Bible whose steps of obedience (Moses, Abraham, Mary, Peter) helped develop their character. Describe that step and what characteristic(s) were fostered.

• What steps of obedience in thought and action have helped you develop something of the character of Jesus in you? Give an example.

- Growth in faith comes through all of the same means that sanctification comes. Above all, growth in faith comes from knowing and meditating on the reality of God and His work for us, in us, and through us; from meditating on the Word of God which reports these things. How can spending time studying and meditating on God's Word help you become what you will yet be?

- And how can—how has and how does—spending time studying and meditating on God's Word help you become what you will yet be?

Faith is the lifeline that connects us to God. Faith is the avenue through which God invades our lives. And faith in God is manifest by actions that are in harmony with our relationship with Him. By faith we pray and seek to hear His voice through the Word and the Spirit. By faith we are obedient to the law of Christ. Indeed, "without faith it is impossible to please God" (Hebrews 11:6).

Father God, teach me to live by Your Spirit, and, Holy Spirit, empower me to live a life which bears fruit for the kingdom and gives glory to the Father. And I ask You now, Lord God, to show me where I am hindering the Spirit's work in my life: show me my sin. . . . And show me, too, what I can do in my prayer life, my Bible study times, and my fellowship to receive more of the Spirit. . . . Most of all, Lord, make me thirsty for Your Spirit that I may know His power to help me be what I am not yet that Your process of sanctifying me may continue. I pray in Jesus' name. Amen.

Growing in Holiness
Through Fellowship

The approach Jesus used when He discipled the Twelve could be summarized as follows: "I'll do it; you come along and watch. Then we will do it together. When I sense that you are ready, I'll let you do it, and I will watch and evaluate. Then you will be commissioned to go into all the world and make disciples. You'll be ready to do the work I taught you." Clearly the key to Jesus' discipling was fellowship.

• When have you personally been discipled by someone? How did you benefit? If you haven't, how might you benefit from such a relationship?

• What benefits come from discipling based in fellowship, as Jesus modeled with the Twelve?

God sanctifies His people when they appropriate His truth by meditating on His Word and obeying it in all that they do. Another vital aspect of Christian growth is fellowship: God conveys Himself and His truth to us through other believers.

The Need for Fellowship (289)

According to Scripture, we are not designed to grow in isolation from other believers; God intends for us to grow together as part of a community. Loving community in the family of God is an integral part of sanctification as well as a means of sanctification.

- What community of believers are you affiliated with? How involved are you? How close do you let yourself get to others?

- Why would fellowship in the family of God be integral to a believer's sanctification?

- When has God clearly used a relationship with a brother or sister in the Lord (fellowship) as a means of sanctification for you?

Fellowship Restores Our True Nature (290)

The relationship between fellowship and growth toward holiness becomes more obvious when we consider our real nature as human persons and how our personal growth is intertwined with that of others.

- In sanctification we not only share in the holiness of God, but also our true nature as human beings is restored. The true nature of our humanity, however, is realized only in community. What experiences in life have helped you realize that it is not good for man to be alone (Genesis 2:18)?

- Our community nature as humans is also evident from the fact that we were created "in the image of [the Triune] God" (Genesis 1:26,27). Explain how "these persons are what they are only in relationship to each other." What does this arrangement, in whose image we were created, suggest about our human nature?

Fellowship Affirms Our Identity (292)

Yet another indication that we were designed to live in fellowship is the realization that our personal identity comes from our relationships. Contrary to the presumption of our Western culture, our individuality is not lost when we become part of a group. Instead we gain our true selfhood by sharing in community.

- When have you noticed the uniqueness of your individual identity emerge in a relationship with another person—or when have you seen that happen to someone you know? Be specific about the uniqueness you saw and, if possible, why it emerged.

- A body part (a toe or kneecap) separated from the body would be a useless blob of flesh. It acquires its identity only in relation to the other parts of the body. What identity have you acquired in relation to others? Be specific about the others and the identity.

Our human nature and divine purpose are not fully realized except in community. This community can be disrupted by sin, but it's only in relation to others—God, our family, and fellow believers—that our personal individuality comes. If we are to grow as a person, we cannot grow in isolation from other people.

Our Oneness in Christ (293)

When we come to Christ personally, we find ourselves one with all others in Him (Galatians 3:28; Ephesians 4:25; Romans 12:5).

Living Out Our Unity (294)

The reality is our unity in Christ: as soon as we are set apart as God's children, we are joined together in Christ by the Spirit.

- Be specific about what you are doing to live out the unity that is a reality in the body. By the power of the Spirit, to whom are you reaching out to and perhaps even feeling connected with that—apart from Christ—you wouldn't?

- Read Ephesians 4:2-6. What specific commands for living out that unity which is a reality do you find here? List them and circle the one you need to work on most.

Becoming One Mature Man (295)

The goal of sanctification is not that we all become perfect individuals or that everyone becomes perfect by themselves. Rather, it is that we all become one "mature man" (Ephesians 4:13 NASB).

- What role does love play in this process?

- What evidence of God's love drawing people into unity do you see where you fellowship?

Together for Eternity (296)

The biblical picture of life in eternity is not one of individual living. What about heaven—and who each believer will be in heaven—will make community there different and better than community we know on earth?

Again, the Bible declares that personal spiritual growth is not designed to take place in isolation, but in close fellowship with a community that is growing together to become one "mature man" of God.

The Role of Relationships (296)

Isolation from the Christian community means no accountability. Sin is inevitable once we start to live independently of God and each other. Also, when we keep other Christians and family members at arm's length, we rob ourselves and others of what God has given to the body of Christ, which can be received only as we relate to one another.

- When has being in fellowship with a body of believers kept you from falling into sin?

- What blessings have you received (or might you receive) by choosing not to keep other Christians, family members, and even God Himself at arm's length?

Relationships and Growth (298)

In Scripture, it is easy to see that spiritual growth means growth in our ability to live in harmony with others. The truth that sanctification or spiritual growth takes place as a result of relationships between believers is also a strong theme in Scripture.

- When have you observed the truth that spiritual growth means growth in our ability to live in harmony with others either in yourself or in others? What role did the fruit of the Spirit (see Galatians 5:22-23) play in that increased harmony?

- When have you been built up or edified by other believers? What kind of spiritual growth have you experienced as a result of being in fellowship with other believers?

Relationships and Bearing Fruit (299)

Look again at Galatians 5:22, 23.
- Which of the fruit of the Spirit needs to be experienced in relationship with another person?

- What does this fact imply about the importance of community?

Relationships and Knowledge (299)

The knowledge of spiritual matters is not gained alone. Rather, it is gained through interaction with other believers (Ephesians 3:18,19).
- When has being in fellowship with believers helped you better "grasp how wide and long and high and deep is the love of Christ" (Ephesians 3:18)? Be specific about how God has loved you through a community of His people.

- When has being in fellowship with believers increased your understanding of spiritual matters? Again, be specific.

Spiritual growth is more than personal; it is communal. God conveys Himself to each of us not only through our personal relations with Him and our practice of the spiritual disciplines, but also through other believers as we fellowship with them.

How Relationships Bring Growth (300)

Now that we understand the truth that fellowship contributes to growth, let's look at the specifics of how this happens.

The Call to Mutual Ministry (300)

Both Ephesians 4 and 1 Corinthians 12 imply that we grow through relationships.

- When exercised, God's gifts of grace to individual believers build up the body of Christ. When have you benefited from people exercising their gifts as, for instance, evangelists and pastor-teacher? What gift(s) do you—or could you—exercise within the body to build it up?

- In a time frame of seven years, every cell in our physical body will die and be replaced except for those in our brain and spinal cord. What does this fact suggest about how all members of the body of Christ are necessary to its life (1 Corinthians 12)?

The Closeness of Mutual Ministry (302)

In Ephesians 4:16 (NASB), Paul describes the body as "being fitted and held together," and, significantly, these verbs are in the present tense, describing continual action.

• What rough edges have been smoothed by God and/or through fellowship with His people so that you could be more solidly joined together with other believers? If you've seen that more clearly in someone else, describe that process and its result.

• When have you needed to reconcile with a fellow believer in order to be "held together" in the body? How did that act of reconciliation help God knit together you and the person involved and perhaps other people as well? Again, describe a personal experience or one you've witnessed.

The Goal of Mutual Ministry (302)

God's goal for humanity is not simply a number of perfected individuals, but a perfected and unified humanity.
• Explain the difference between these two possible goals and the benefits of the latter.

• Why would a perfected and unified humanity result in more glory to God than a number of perfected individuals? Consider the point of George T. Montague on page 303.

Spiritual growth is at once personal and communal, and the source of all growth is God Himself communicated through His Son and empowered by His Spirit.

The Means of Encouraging Growth (303)

How does the communication of Christ's life and our spiritual growth actually take place in the fellowship of believers?

- The practice of the "one anothers" in the New Testament is one way. When have you experienced the following (either giving or receiving)—and what kind of personal and/or communal growth resulted?

  Encouragement

  Being spurred on to love and good deeds

  Comfort

  Admonishment

  Being served in love

  Having others help you carry your burdens

  Confessing your sins and being prayed for

One important way we can minister to each other is through prayer and even singing.

- When have you been helped by someone praying for you?

• When have you experienced community growth in a time of group prayer? Describe what happened.

• What role does prayer—private as well as corporate—play in your spiritual walk? Consider how much time you regularly commit to prayer.

• When has corporate singing with a body of believers encouraged your spiritual growth?

• When have you been ministered to in the following ways—and what regular opportunities do you have to minister to others in each of these ways?

Doing good

Practicing hospitality

Corporate giving

We can learn much about the means of encouraging growth from the early church: the people "committed themselves to the teaching of the apostles, the life together, the common meal, and the prayers" (Acts 2:42 *The Message*).

The Benefits of Fellowship (305)

In the fellowship of believer with believer, the supernatural life of Christ is shared through the power of the Spirit. It is because of Christ's life that we receive spiritual nourishment when we are with one another.

Fellowship Provides Strength (305)

There is a strengthening of faith when it is shared in common with others.

- The world bombards us with its lies. When has fellowship helped you personally stand strong against those lies? Consider, for instance, the world's value system, its lies about what really matters.

- Remember how the Roman soldiers held their door-shaped body shields together for corporate protection? What issues in the world does your fellowship of believers take a strong stand against corporately?

Fellowship Provides Learning (305)

Learning is another aspect of spiritual growth that best takes place in the context of Christian fellowship.

- When have you benefited from the teaching or insights of a fellow believer? Give specific examples about the lesson(s) learned.

- When in a fellowship situation have you seen an aspect of God's truth modeled? Again, give specific examples about the lesson(s) learned. Comment on the significance of seeing the truth modeled rather than simply reading about it.

- What role does fellowship play in what you are learning about your faith? Consider how much time you regularly commit to Bible studies or adult Sunday school.

Fellowship Provides Accountability (306)

Isolation is a great breeding ground for sin; fellowship and the accountability it offers serves as a powerful antidote.

- How has or does fellowship keep you from sin? Be specific about the Christian accountability systems in your life.

- As Michael Griffiths points out about Christian community, "We sometimes help each other because we are easy and beautiful to live with. We sometimes help each other because we are difficult to live with and quite unintentionally, therefore, we sanctify one another!"[1] When has Christian community helped you by being "easy and beautiful to live with," perhaps a place of healing and encouragement and prayer when you were unable to pray for yourself? Be specific.

• When has your fellowship with believers helped you by being "difficult to live with"? How did God use them to help you become more like Christ?

Fellowship with other believers provides strength, learning, and accountability as well as much joy and immeasurable blessing.

The Preeminence of Relationships (306)

God works in our lives primarily through committed relationships. Consider the progression of Paul's logic in Colossians: he presents the finished work of Christ, then he talks about establishing God's people in Christ, and finally he discusses moving Christians on toward maturity and all of his instructions about character are relationship-oriented.

• If you're not in fellowship with believers, summarize what you may be missing out on.

• If you're not in fellowship with believers, why aren't you? What obstacles keep you isolated? What will you do—starting today—to overcome those obstacles?

Our sanctification happens in the context of relationships—and love binds us all together as we grow (Colossians 3:14).

The Keys to Great Fellowship (307)

Someone once said that living in the context of committed relationships is like living in Noah's ark: "We wouldn't be able to stand the stink inside if it weren't for the storm outside!" Living together would be much easier if we all fulfilled two key responsibilities.

- We must all take responsibility for our character. What are you doing to conform—and to let God work in your life to conform you—to Christ's character? Be specific.

- We must also love one another. Whom do you need to be asking God to help you be more accepting of? In general, how willing are you to lay down your life for another? Make that a topic of prayer as well.

Imagine what would happen in our homes and churches if everybody assumed their responsibility for their own growth in character and everybody made a commitment to meet another's needs! Our homes and churches would be more like heaven than Noah's ark—and we would all be more like Jesus!

Almighty God, I thank You that, while I can't be discipled directly by the physical presence of Jesus, I can be discipled by His people. Thank You that You convey Yourself—Your love and grace, Your hope and truth—to us through other believers. And I thank You that fellowship with other believers restores our true nature and affirms our identity. Enable me to be willing to take responsibility for my own character and willing to love one another so that I may be a contributing member of the Christian community. Enable me to be willing to both be sharpened and to be used to sharpen others. Finally, I praise You for the blessings and potential blessings of being in fellowship with Your people—the blessings of strength, learning, accountability, joy, and love. In Jesus' name. Amen.

The COMMON MADE HOLY

16

The Struggle of Sanctification

Every child of God is a diamond in the rough, but we begin our Christian walk looking more like a lump of coal. Staying pure and remaining under pressure is what makes a diamond out of coal. The same is true for us as Christians, but the process of Christian growth is far more than a restful passivity.

A Determined Pursuit (310)

Working out our salvation is a rigorous process that involves sacrifice and suffering. Read again "Coach" Paul's words in 1 Corinthians 9:24-27 and then evaluate how much effort you are putting in to working out your salvation.

- What is your "spring training" program? What do you do to keep up on the basics of your faith? What could you be doing to stay sharp?

Sanctification requires us to ground ourselves in the basics of our faith and then discipline ourselves to live according to what God says is true.

An Ongoing Battle (311)

Whether we like it or not, we are in a battle against evil forces (Ephesians 6:10-16). At the cross, Christ won the decisive battle over the powers of sin, but the defeated enemies have not yet been totally eradicated. In a real sense, the battleground is now in our lives.

• What metaphors and images for the Christian life does Paul use in the following passages?

1 Timothy 1:18

1 Timothy 6:11,12

2 Timothy 2:3

2 Timothy 4:7

• When have you noticed that the closer we grow to Christ, the more the battle against evil forces is likely to intensify? Be specific about a struggle you have either experienced or witnessed.

• What growth have you experienced as you've struggled with the impersonal effects of sin—such as the suffering that comes with physical disease, grief and death?

The Flesh: The Traitor Within (312)

One of the opponents of our Christian growth is within us. Our "flesh" has sinful desires which are antithetical to those of the Spirit of God within us as well as to us and our sanctification (Romans 7:25; Galatians 5:16; 1 Peter 2:11).

Defining the Flesh (313)

• Address its various aspects as you summarize the definition of "flesh."

Breaking the Power of the Flesh (314)

• Having read this section, answer the question which many Christians have: If the flesh has been crucified, why do we still have trouble with it? Do so in terms of "already" and "not yet."

What the Flesh Does (316)

• A legalistic life of religiosity and good works *and* an immoral, lawless, pleasure-seeking life are both fleshly. In what area(s) of life does the flesh tempt you to enthrone self and live autonomously? Be specific.

Correctly Responding to the Flesh (318)

• When did you first realize that you are powerless against sin without Christ?

• What does the chart on page 317 help clarify about the struggle we have against the flesh?

The flesh is the constant propensity to avoid either living life through the cross or gaining true life through giving up our self-centeredness. We cannot resist the flesh on our own. Living by the flesh we are powerless against sin. We must depend upon the Spirit as we resist the flesh and seek the things above.

Resisting the Flesh (319)

The Spirit is the power by which the evil desires of the flesh can be resisted, but we have to participate with Him.

- What practices which you know are sinful have been or even continue to be an area of struggle?

- How has (or does or could) the Spirit help you in the areas you've identified?

- What do you do in your daily life to take every thought captive to the obedience of Christ (2 Corinthians 10:5)?

- How does (or could) your thought life, centered in Christ, help you resist the flesh? Be specific.

Seek the Things Above (319)

The other action we are to take against the flesh is to "set your mind on the things above" (Colossians 3:2 NASB). If we mentally focus on earthly things, we will likely carry out the desires of the flesh.

Replacing Fleshly Thoughts with Truth (321)

- What about the truth and the character of Christ helps you see the ugliness of the flesh? Be specific and worshipful as you consider your Lord and Savior.

- Which of the characteristics you just listed will you choose to think about the next time you face temptation?

Avoiding Fleshly Situations (322)

- What tangible provisions for the desires of the flesh do you need to get rid of? What will you do when you find yourself entertaining thoughts and plans for carrying out these desires in secret?

- What compromising situations do you need to avoid? Be specific as, in the power of the Spirit, you renounce them.

• What role can and, ideally, does fellowship with the body of believers play in helping you resist the flesh and seek the things above?

The World: Opposition from Outside (322)

Not only do we have to contend with the flesh, but we also need to stand against the world.

Defining the World (322)

• Address its various aspects as you summarize the definition of "world."

The Elements of Worldliness (323)

• What does each of the following elements refer to? After you define each element, identify specific occasions when you contend with these lusts and sources of pride.

Lusts of the flesh

Lusts of the eyes

The boastful pride of life

- To determine how worldly your life is, simply answer the question, "Is God included in all that you do and do you do all things to please Him?" What does your answer teach you about yourself?

Friendship with God or the World? (325)

The world constantly seeks to pull our love away from Christ by appealing to our flesh, which desires to live after the world's values. In what aspects of your life are you tempted to be a friend with the world? What, for instance, do you find yourself praying about? Put differently, what motivates certain prayers—a desire to satisfy your pleasures or a seeking after what pleases God?

Correctly Responding to the World (325)

- What sources of the world's call to self-sufficiency are loudest in your life? In what area(s) of your life is that call most compelling?

- Our initial faith in Christ made us overcomers, and our continuing faith in Christ wins the battle on a daily basis. In practical terms, how does your faith in Christ help you be victorious in that daily battle?

Before having the presence of God in our lives or any knowledge of His ways, our minds were programmed by the world, which conditioned our flesh to live our lives independent of God. Because we as Christians still live in the world, it can continue to shape us.

Faith's Role in Overcoming the World (327)

• Faith in Christ means faith in the cross. Why does the world hate the cross? And why does the believer love the cross?

• What are you doing to fuel your love of the cross, to strengthen your faith that overcomes the world?

• In simple terms, resistance to the world is right-mindedness, and worldliness is the epitome of ignorance. To love the world is to deliberately plan for doom (1 John 2:17).

Making the Right Choice (328)

As the choice of the rich young ruler indicates (Matthew 19), it isn't easy to give up the false security and fleshly indulgences of this world.

- Look again at Jesus' words in Matthew 18:2-4. Why is childlike humility key to entering the kingdom of heaven and standing strong against the world?

- Is your ladder to success leaning on the right wall? Support your answer with specific evidence from your life.

The world and the flesh are formidable foes that we cannot take lightly. We need to stand strong in the Spirit. As we do, we can be assured that any position in the world pales in comparison to being seated with Christ in the heavenlies.

Almighty God, I know that, in You, ultimate victory is certain, but I am very aware that the present battle rages. You, Creator God, know the flesh: You know the temptation I face to enthrone myself and live autonomously. Thank You for providing Your Spirit as a source of strength for me to resist the flesh; teach me to rely on Him . . . Thank You for providing Your Word as a source of truth as I seek the things above; help me become more a student of the Word . . . And thank You for providing the body of believers who strengthen me for the battle; help me be open with them so they can indeed help me . . . Finally, grant me a clear vision of Jesus as I struggle to resist the lusts of the flesh, the lusts of the eyes, and the boastful pride of life and instead strive to follow Him. It is in His name I pray. Amen.

The COMMON MADE HOLY

17

The Warfare of Sanctification

The flesh and the world are two enemies of sanctification. The third and ultimate enemy is the very real spiritual force of evil.

Engaged in a Real Battle (332)

The one who lies behind and utilizes both the world and the flesh in his opposition against the plan of God is "the ruler of this world" (John 14:30 NASB), the "prince of the power of the air" (Ephesians 2:2 NASB).

- What does Ephesians 6:12 teach about the nature of the battle believers face in this life? To what degree do you know this truth in a practical sense? Put differently, how do you deal with the reality of this battle in your day-to-day life?

• According to 2 Corinthians 4:4, why may some people never receive the abundant life that Jesus offered? What, if anything, is keeping you from experiencing that life?

The real battle is between the Christ and the antichrist; between the One who is truth and the father of lies; between the kingdom of light and the kingdom of darkness; between the Spirit of truth and deceiving spirits; and ultimately between life and death.

Acknowledging a Real Enemy (333)

Belief in a personal devil has always been part of the doctrinal statement of the historical church.

• In 1 Peter 5:8, what picture of the enemy does Peter paint?

• Just before His arrest, Jesus warned His disciples that Satan was going to try to destroy their faith (Luke 22:31). When have you been aware of Satan's efforts to destroy your faith? Be specific about the struggle.

Satan's goal is nothing less than the devouring of believers, and to reach that goal Satan uses various schemes.

Satan's Schemes (333)

Consider now some of your enemy's schemes.

Temptation Through Deception (333)

True life and growth come from incorporating God's life into our lives via faith in His Word, His truth. The opposite is also true: Death and destruction come from that which opposes God—the lie.

- When has the devil tempted you to believe and consequently live out his lies? Be specific about the lies.

It Began with a Lie (334)

- All temptation is an attempt to get us to live our lives independent of God. To do that, Satan tries to get us to doubt God's infinite love and goodness and to believe that God is somehow limiting the fullness of our lives. Comment on how these facts fit with the lie(s) you just identified.

A Crafty Enemy (335)

- Thomas Brooks wrote about many of Satan's clever strategies. Which of those (listed on page 336) have you experienced and even fallen victim to? How did you respond to the accusations that came once you gave in to temptation?

Satan Knows Our Weaknesses (336)

- Brooks also points out how Satan, with his superhuman knowledge, can tailor temptation to each of us. Review the examples he gives (page 337). In what areas does Satan tend to tempt you? What about these points suggests that his strategy is tailor-made for you?

Temptation Through the World System (337)

Many of Satan's temptations are mediated through others in the world system about us. That was the case for Jesus (Luke 4).

- Satan directly assaulted Jesus in the wilderness. But what is significant about the last phrase of Luke 4:13 and how does that give credence to Hebrews 4:15?

- Which of the following sources of temptation have you encountered?

  Worldliness

  Pride

  Persecution

  Physical pain

  Emotional hurt

- With each of these experiences, what were you tempted to believe or disbelieve about God?

Deception Through Direct Thoughts (339)

Satan can also deceive us by putting certain thoughts in our minds.

- What, if anything, in this discussion is new to you? What did the examples of David and Judas and the testimony of Martin Luther reveal to you?

- What of the following struggles have you experienced?

  Difficulty concentrating on and reading the Bible

  Actually hearing "voices"

  Accusing or condemning thoughts

  Blasphemous ideas

• Summarize what the deceiver was attempting in these struggles.

Deception Through False Teachers (341)

Demons are also behind false teachings that lead believers from the truth (1 Timothy 4:1; 2 Timothy 2:25,26). It is possible that Paul viewed evil spirits as also being behind legalistic teachings that hold people in bondage.

• One telltale sign of some false prophets is that they "despise authority" (2 Peter 2:10). Why would that be the case?

• Which of the following, if any, have you encountered and struggled against?

False teachers who oppose God's truth

Legalistic teachings that hold people in bondage

False prophets

• What tool does God provide to help you stand against false teachers? What are you doing to "gird your loins with truth" (Ephesians 6:14)?

Deception Through Physical Attacks and Miracles (342)

At least 25 percent of all the healings recorded in the Gospels are actually the result of the Lord freeing people from spiritual attacks.

- The Lord didn't free Paul from the "messenger of Satan" (2 Corinthians 12:7), but what did He do? How did He use its presence for Paul's good, for the apostle's sanctification?

- When have you been aware of seeing (or even experiencing) physical attack by the devil and/or false miracles? What is Satan's goal in these deceptions? Consider the words of Irenaeus (pages 342-343).

- So how does Satan's work of deception relate to the attacks of our other enemies—the world and the flesh?

Satan, the Flesh, and the World (343)

- Is Satan the cause of our temptations, or is the world, or our own sinful flesh?

Three Sources of Temptation (343)

Scripture reveals that it is difficult—if not impossible—to sep-arate the temptations that arise from Satan, the flesh, and the world, and to do so may be erroneous.

- What does Ephesians 2:2-3 suggest about the relation-ship of Satan, the flesh, and the world? See also James 1:14,15 and 4:4-6.

- Look again at the summary paragraph on page 344. What insight into the warfare of sanctification do these state-ments give you? What encouragement to stand strong in the Spirit do you find here?

Who Is Ultimately Responsible? (344)

Even though three enemies are involved in attempting to pull us away from God, it is important to note that the final respon-sibility for our sin rests on us.

- What promise do you find in 1 Corinthians 10:13?

• Consider two or three specific instances of temptation to sin which you have faced. What way of escape did God provide in each instance? Did you choose that path or the path of sin? Why?

As believers in Christ, we are indwelt by the Spirit of God and freed from the bondage of sin, but we must make the responsible choice to serve our Lord rather than give in to the temptations to sin.

The Extent of Satan's Attacks (345)

We as Christians are no longer in the kingdom of darkness and are freed from Satan's power, but we can still enslave ourselves by the choices we make.

• What do the following passages teach about the security of a believer's position in Christ?

Acts 26:18

Romans 8:38,39

Ephesians 6a:11-18

Opening Ourselves to Satan's Influence (346)

Scripture, however, indicates that believers can still give themselves over to sin and evil powers and become enslaved to them.

- What lesson on man's susceptibility to Satan's influence does Ananias offer? See Acts 5:1-11 and Richard Rackham's discussion on pages 346-347.

- What are you doing—or could you be doing—to be sure you are influenced by God's Spirit rather than Satan's demons? Be specific.

Even Christians Are Susceptible (347)

Christians, even good ones, can be deceived by Satan and trapped by evil.

- Satan can use our anger to trap us. When has that been your experience, or when have you seen that principle illustrated in a believer's life?

- How is Satan using long-held anger, resentment, or lack of forgiveness to hold you in bondage today? What would God have you do to get out of that trap?

Some Crucial Distinctions (349)

- How far can the enslavement of believers go? Can it include their actual demonization?

Defining the Terms (349)

- First consider the terminology. Why is "demonized" a better term than "possession"?

Responding to an Objection (350)

- Some Christians object to the idea that believers can be internally affected by a demon. Summarize the two objections to this presented in the text.

Examining the Possibilities (350)

- What evidence have you seen that believers can allow sinful practices to dominate their lives?

- Having read this section, do you think a believer could sinfully come under the control of an evil spirit? Why or why not?

Attack from personal evil spirits is usually related to the sins that stem from the evil desires of our own flesh. Satan takes advantage of our weak, sinful flesh to push his influence over us.

Correctly Responding to Satanic Attacks (353)

- Yielding to the flesh is also yielding to the influences of Satan and his demons. How are we to effectively respond to these influences and attacks?

Repenting of Our Sins (353)

If we find that we have succumbed to Satan's influence, our first response has to be repentance (2 Timothy 2:25,26).

- Why can repentance be a difficult step? Consider whose influence you are trying to escape as well as your own human pride.

- Is repentance a step you need to take today? If so, do it—and get the help of another person if you need to.

Taking a Stand in the Faith (353)

When we're faced with satanic attacks, the critical issue is our relationship with God. Once that is established, we can stand against the evil one.

• What promises do you find in James 4:7 and 1 Peter 5:9?

• We must actively take our place in Christ. What do you do regularly to put on the armor of God? Give specifics for each item listed in Ephesians 6:13-15.

Choosing the Truth (354)

Choosing the truth is our first line of defense: "we take captive every thought to make it obedient to Christ" (2 Corinthians 10:5).

• Why is it a dangerous waste of time to analyze whether a thought comes from the television, another person, our own memories, or the pit?

• What is the difference between dispelling the darkness and turning to the light? Which are you, as a believer, called to do?

Making Ourselves Humble (355)

Commitment to God means making ourselves low before Him (James 4:6; 1 Peter 5:5).

- Humility is confidence properly placed. In whom can and should believers place their confidence? Why?

- Read what Thomas Brooks said about humility (page 355). What images help you appreciate the importance of humility?

Arming Ourselves with Spiritual Weapons (355)

Spiritual warfare against spiritual foes requires spiritual weapons.

- What spiritual weapon did Jesus Himself rely on in His battle against Satan? See Matthew 4:1-11.

- Spiritual warfare rests on communion with God and His power. What do you do to stay in communion with God in your day-to-day life? When has that communion provided the power you needed to stand against Satan? Give a specific example or two.

Remembering That Victory Is Assured (356)

We should be comforted in the knowledge that Satan's attacks have limitations.

- Satan needs permission from two sources. What are they?

- What hope do you find in the fact that we don't fight the battle in our own strength and in the truths of John 16:33 and 1 Corinthians 15:57?

As we stand firm in our faith at the end of the twentieth century, we stand with the early church fathers. Hear—and find encouragement in—what Tertullian wrote: "All the authority and power we have over [demons] is from naming the name of Christ, and recalling to their memory the woes with which God threatens them. . . . Fearing Christ in God, and God in Christ, they become subject to the servants of God and Christ." Amen.[1]

Almighty God, I've found in this chapter many reminders that, as Your child, I am engaged in a real battle. And, from experience, I know all too well Satan's efforts to deceive and his strategies of deception. So I find great hope in Your promise to help me overcome when I'm tempted (1 Corinthians 10:13). In order to stand against him, I ask You to help me acknowledge, confess, and repent of my sins . . . Give me the ability to recognize and choose truth . . . Help me place my confidence in You, not in myself or the solutions of the world . . . Thank You for the weapons You have provided and for the fact that I can rest in the truth that victory is assured in Christ. . . . In the meantime, Lord, I want to be abiding in Christ and walking by Your Spirit. I pray in Jesus' name. Amen.

The COMMON MADE HOLY

18

The Suffering and Triumph in Sanctification

Practicing the Christian life begins with being a good steward of everything that God has entrusted to us, including our own lives. But we can commit to God only what we know about ourselves, which is not everything there is to know.

God will reveal our hearts at the final judgment on the Day of the Lord. But the revealing of our hearts also takes place in our present lives.

- When have you echoed the psalmist's prayer, "Search me, O God, and know my heart" (Psalm 139:23) and had Him reveal something you hadn't realized about yourself? What specifically did you learn about yourself?

- When has God's Word revealed your heart to yourself? Give one or two specific instances.

Christian maturity includes the process of God revealing to us our unconscious thoughts or the unconscious contents of the soul.

Growth and Transparency (361)

Turn to page 361 and the diagram of the Christian. Keep in mind that we are talking about character—who we are rather than what we do.

Our Christian growth will always be inhibited to the degree that we cover up who we really are.

- In what areas of your life are you more concerned with how you look to other people rather than to God?

- When has a brother or sister in the Lord helped you recognize aspects of yourself that you were blind to? What were those blind spots?

- Explain the difference between judgment and discipline by clarifying what each focuses on. What does this difference tell you about the blind spots you might feel called to point out in another person?

- God intends for us to speak the truth in love—with a love that communicates acceptance—as we help each other recognize our blind spots. When has another believer's love and acceptance freed you to grow?

In 1 Corinthians 4:3-5, Paul says that we shouldn't be concerned about what others think of us because the One who examines us is the Lord.

- Are you concerned about what others think? Do you, like Paul when he wrote these words to the Corinthians, have nothing against yourself? Are you on a plateau right now?

- Perhaps rather than being on a plateau, you need to take some time for prayerful soul-searching. Do so now and let Psalm 139:23,24 guide you.

Plateaus are the good times in the process of being sanctified. We don't feel convicted by anything, and our conscience is clean. But plateaus don't last forever.

Growth and Suffering (363)

Plateaus end because God has a way of letting us know that we are not yet qualified to be a member of the Trinity!

Usually the way we interact with people reveals how stubborn and immature we really are.

- Which of the following ways do you tend to respond to the reproofs of life and God's Word?

Drop out

Hang in there but never grow up

Own up to your "something less than Christlike character"

• Why do people struggle to admit their mistakes and agree with God that perfection has eluded them?

God's Design in Suffering (364)

Paul could exult in his tribulations (Romans 5:3-5) because he knew we have a God of hope. We can rely on Him as we undergo the process of sanctification, a process which involves warfare and therefore suffering.

• God's intention is that we come through the trials and tribulations of life a better person than we were before. Give a biblical example of that happening... a real-life example of someone you know or know of... and an example of a situation from your own life which God used to help you become a better person.

• When, if at all, has God used an earthquake (metaphorically speaking) to get your attention—or could one be coming because you have resisted God's process of sanctification? If you have experienced an earthquake, talk about what happened and what you learned. If you suspect one could be coming, confess to God where you've been god in your life and repent of your sinfulness.

• The suffering we face as we grow from sin toward holiness is inevitable. What comfort do you find in the fact that Paul and even Jesus Himself suffered? What reason for rejoicing can you find in suffering? See Acts 5:41 for one possibility.

The Necessity of Suffering (367)

In the words of J.I. Packer, "suffering Christianly is an integral aspect of biblical holiness, and a regular part of business as usual for the believer."[1]

• What do the following passages teach about the necessity of suffering?
Romans 8:17

2 Corinthians 1:5

2 Timothy 2:9-12

• Which of the following sources of suffering have you encountered? At this point, what do you realize about how God used these experiences to grow you toward holiness?
Result of living in a hostile world

Chastisement from God when we're involved in sin

Human frailty

Broken love

The Value of Suffering (369)

Despite our natural aversion to suffering, Scripture tells us that we can expect suffering and, in fact, it is a necessity for spiritual growth.

Suffering Motivates Change (369)

- Pain—physical or spiritual—is a warning that further deterioration is inevitable unless something is changed. When has pain served that purpose in your life—or the life of someone you know? What change (toward holiness) resulted?

Suffering Builds Righteous Character (369)

- List the various effects that suffering had on Jesus. Which of these have you experienced as a result of suffering? Be specific about the experience.

- What is the connection between learning to love (dying to self) and suffering, with all it can teach?

Suffering Draws Us to God (370)

- Complete holiness is to love God Himself (not what He gives us) with all our heart. When have you let suffering draw you to God? What was the alternative? What were the benefits of turning to the Lord?

Suffering Helps Us Understand God (371)

- Answer the question "Why does suffering help us understand God?" by explaining what has caused God to suffer.

Suffering Promotes Ministry and Unity (371)

- When have you found that suffering promotes ministry and unity? Talk about both sides: giving and receiving blessing through service.

- Our suffering can serve God by bringing Him glory. When have you seen God's sustaining grace in the life of someone who suffered? What benefits did you receive from that witness?

Our Response to Suffering (372)

Suffering is inevitable in our fallen and anti-Christian world that is conditioned by sin. Therefore we shouldn't be surprised when we experience physical, emotional, and spiritual pain.

Three Key Truths (372)

Paul writes, "everyone who wants to live a godly life in Christ Jesus will be persecuted" (2 Timothy 3:12), and the proper response to that is to let suffering work toward our sanctification. Which of the following truths have you clung to?

1. *God is always in control of our suffering.*

   What characteristics of God enable you to find hope in this fact?

2. *God always has a limit on the amount of suffering He allows for each of us (1 Corinthians 10:13).*

   When has God's grace enabled you to bear up under pain? Thank Him for that.

3. *God will always provide "a way out" so that we can "stand up under" our suffering.*

   Consider a time of pain and suffering you've experienced. What was the "way out" God provided?

A *Key Promise* (374)

- In what ways have you experienced the comfort of God, "the Father of compassion and the God of all comfort, who comforts us in all our troubles" (2 Corinthians 1:3,4)?

Rejoicing in Our Sufferings (375)

James calls us to "Consider it pure joy . . . whenever you face trials of many kinds" (James 1:2; see also Romans 5:3 and 1 Peter 4:13).

- We aren't called to rejoice because of the suffering itself or in the sense of seeking more suffering. Why can we be joyful despite and in the midst of our sufferings?

- When have you experienced God's strength and comfort as suffering revealed your weakness? Be specific.

- The right attitude in suffering is to focus on the hope that is before us, hope that fuels our joy. What hope do you find in Revelation 21:4? And when, like me (Robert), have you found a certain sweetness of joy even when your heart was filled with indescribable pain?

When Suffering Comes (378)

- In Isaiah 50:10,11, the prophet talks about a believer who obeys God yet walks in darkness—not the darkness of sin or the kingdom of darkness, but the darkness of uncertainty that comes when God suspends His conscious blessings. What should we do when we find ourselves in such oppressive circumstances?

Keep on Walking (379)

• What evidence of God's faithfulness in your past can be touchstones for times of darkness you may encounter? Be specific and refer to this list when suffering comes.

• When in a time of darkness has nothing changed circumstantially but everything changed internally? Why did this keep you walking? What did this change teach you about God?

• Review God's questions to me (Neil) at the bottom of page 380. What do these questions show you about the substance and focus of your faith?

Walk in God's Light Only (382)

• We are not to create our own light when dark times come; we aren't to resort to doing things our way. Consider the ongoing consequences of Abraham and Sarah's efforts and the forty years in the desert Moses experienced. When has misery followed your attempt to do things your way?

- If you've experienced the darkness that can come with suffering, talk about a time morning came and that darkness ended. Had you reached the bottom? What was the source of hope? What realization about God or Jesus or yourself or your calling as a believer did you come to at this moment?

- What have you learned about compassion in God's ministry of darkness? When have you been able to use what you've learned to come alongside others? Give an example or two.

- When has a time of darkness brought you to the end of your resources so you could discover God's resources? Be specific about the experience and especially about what you learned about God.

- How have your times of suffering and darkness helped you die to yourself, a key aspect of sanctification? Be specific.

Trust God Completely (386)

• Yet another reason that God allows us to walk in darkness is to help us learn to trust Him, and we can trust that He is using the suffering we encounter to grow us into Christlikeness. Consider the greatest times of growth in your life. Have they been a time of testing? Why are growth and suffering often connected?

• Possibly the greatest sign of spiritual maturity is the ability to postpone rewards (Hebrews 11:13,39). What rewards of eternity have given you hope to hold on to during your dark days?

God makes everything right in the end, yet our reward may not be in this lifetime, as it wasn't for many of the heroes mentioned in Hebrews 11. Yet I believe with all my heart that when our life on earth is done, all those who have remained faithful will say that the will of God is good, acceptable, and perfect (Romans 12:2).

Growth and God's Reward (387)

If I had known beforehand what my family would have to go through to get where we are today, I probably wouldn't have come this way. But looking back, we all say, "We're glad God took us down the paths that He did."

• Why is it a touch of grace that God doesn't show us what's on the other side of the door as we journey through life?

Suffering is the crucible in which faith and confidence in God are developed. Suffering for the sake of righteousness is intended to make us into the people that God wants us to be.

- What biblical figure gained faith and confidence in God on the crucible of suffering?

- What believer in your life is a living example of a person who has gained faith and confidence in God through suffering?

- Finally, in response to the call in Hebrews 10:32-39, look back on previous times of your own suffering. What about that experience and the lessons learned, the faith and confidence in God which developed, will help you when suffering comes again?

We as Christians are called to willingly accept the Refiner's fire . . . so that we who are common may become holy. Like Him.

Almighty, Sovereign, and Holy God, I praise You for Your unfailing love, Your perfect plan, and the hope and comfort I find in You and in the fact that You know pain. I praise You, too, for the fact that You use and redeem the suffering of my life and for the ways You've sustained me in the past. When trials, pain, suffering come again, may I cast my cares upon You and once again know Your grace (Psalm 55:22). And, Lord, help me never to doubt in darkness what I have learned in the light about You and Your goodness. Help me also to cling to the hope I have in You so that I will remain faithful and one day see that Your will is indeed good, acceptable, and perfect (Romans 12:2). Most of all, Lord, help me to willingly accept Your Refiner's fire . . . so that I may indeed become holy like you. I pray in the name of Your Holy Son. Amen.

NOTES

GOD'S DESIRE FOR YOU

1. The lyrics from the song "Refiner's Fire," written by Brian Doerksen, are used by permission from Mercy/Vineyard Publishing, ©1990.

CHAPTER TWO

1. Georg Fohrer, *Theological Dictionary of the New Testament*, edited by Gerhard Friedrich, vol. 7 (Grand Rapids: Eerdmans, 1971), p. 973.

CHAPTER THREE

1. Chris Brain and Robert Warren, "Why Revival Really Tarries Holiness," *Renewal* (June 1991), p. 35; cited by J.I. Packer, *Rediscovering Holiness* (Ann Arbor, MI: Servant Publications, 1992), pp. 27-28.

CHAPTER FOUR

1. Horatius Bonar, *God's Way of Holiness* (New York: Robert Carter & Brothers, 1865), p. 58.

CHAPTER FIVE

1. Robert Jewett, *Paul's Anthropological Terms* (Leiden: E.J. Brill, 1971), pp. 322-23.

CHAPTER SIX

1. Andrew T. Lincoln, *Ephesians*, Word Biblical Commentary, vol. 42 (Dallas: Word Books, 1990), pp. 285-86.

2. Markus Barth, *Ephesians 4-6*, The Anchor Bible (Garden City, NY: Doubleday & Co., 1974), p. 454.

CHAPTER SEVEN

1. Robert Durback, ed., *Seed of Hope, A Henri Nouwen Reader* (New York: Bantam Books, 1990), p. 197.

CHAPTER NINE

1. John Eadie, *Commentary on the Epistle to the Ephesians* (Grand Rapids: Zondervan, n.d., rpt. of 1883 edition, T. & T. Clark), p. 346.

CHAPTER TEN

1. *Steps to Freedom in Christ*, available from Freedom in Christ Ministries, 1-562-691-9128.

2. Horatius Bonar, *God's Way of Holiness* (New York: Robert Carter & Brothers, 1865), pp. 197-198.

CHAPTER ELEVEN

1. Peter T. O'Brien, *Colossians, Philemon*, The Word Biblical Commentary, vol. 44 (Waco, TX: Word, 1982), p. 23.

CHAPTER TWELVE

1. Peter C. Craige, *The Book of Deuteronomy*, New International Commentary on the Old Testament (Grand Rapids: Eerdman's, 1976), p. 170.

CHAPTER FOURTEEN

1. John White, *The Fight* (Downers Grove, IL: InterVarsity Press, 1976), p. 98.

2. Walter Marshall, *The Gospel-Mystery of Sanctification* (Grand Rapids: Zondervan, 1954), p. 172.

3. See C.S. Lewis, *Mere Christianity* (New York: Macmillan, 1960), pp. 146-151.

CHAPTER FIFTEEN

1. Michael Griffiths, *God's Forgetful Pilgrims* (Grand Rapids: Eerdmans, 1975), p. 65.

CHAPTER SEVENTEEN

1. In Everett Ferguson, *Demonology of the Early Christian World* (New York: The Edwin Mellen Press, 1984), pp. 130-131.

CHAPTER EIGHTEEN

1. J.I. Packer, *Rediscovering Holiness* (Ann Arbor, MI: Servant Publications, 1992), p. 250.